Exploring Leadership D

To Kapil,

Best wishes,

Ian c Woodward

April 2019

Ian C. Woodward • Samah Shaffakat
Vincent H. Dominé

# Exploring Leadership Drivers and Blockers

Ian C. Woodward  
Professor of Management Practice  
INSEAD  
Asia Campus, Singapore

Samah Shaffakat  
Senior Lecturer  
Liverpool Business School  
Liverpool, UK

Vincent H. Dominé  
Adjunct Professor of Leadership  
INSEAD  
Fontainebleau, France

ISBN 978-981-13-6275-0   ISBN 978-981-13-6276-7  (eBook)  
https://doi.org/10.1007/978-981-13-6276-7

Library of Congress Control Number: 2019934465

© The Editor(s) (if applicable) and The Author(s), under exclusive licence to Springer Nature Singapore Pte Ltd. 2019
This work is subject to copyright. All rights are solely and exclusively licensed by the Publisher, whether the whole or part of the material is concerned, specifically the rights of translation, reprinting, reuse of illustrations, recitation, broadcasting, reproduction on microfilms or in any other physical way, and transmission or information storage and retrieval, electronic adaptation, computer software, or by similar or dissimilar methodology now known or hereafter developed.
The use of general descriptive names, registered names, trademarks, service marks, etc. in this publication does not imply, even in the absence of a specific statement, that such names are exempt from the relevant protective laws and regulations and therefore free for general use.
The publisher, the authors and the editors are safe to assume that the advice and information in this book are believed to be true and accurate at the date of publication. Neither the publisher nor the authors or the editors give a warranty, express or implied, with respect to the material contained herein or for any errors or omissions that may have been made. The publisher remains neutral with regard to jurisdictional claims in published maps and institutional affiliations.

Cover Image: © Science Photo Library / Alamy Stock Photo

This Palgrave Macmillan imprint is published by the registered company Springer Nature Singapore Pte Ltd.
The registered company address is: 152 Beach Road, #21-01/04 Gateway East, Singapore 189721, Singapore

**Keywords** Leadership development • Self-awareness • Conscious and unconscious • Drivers • Blockers • Drivers and blockers • Immunity to change • Insightfully aware leadership • Leadership transformation • Individual change • Leadership development objectives • Coaching approaches and tools

# Preface

The three of us share a commitment to helping leaders to achieve transformation and become the "best version" of themselves that they can imagine. Through our leadership development research, teaching and coaching work over the past decade, we have become increasingly interested in examining ways to accelerate leadership development change and to increase levels of profound self-awareness.

So, our book—***Exploring Leadership Drivers and Blockers***—is a multi-author monograph, presenting research on one area that we have seen as increasingly important in our leadership development and change support mission. This is the idea of exploring both conscious and unconscious ***drivers and blockers*** related to a leader's development objectives and their personal change or leadership transformation efforts.

In the book, we argue that exploring drivers and blockers is a prerequisite to enhanced and profound levels of self-awareness. Drivers are those "assumptions" and "forces" in people that create, promote and power activity, as well as give impetus and desire to personal change action. Drivers guide and sustain objectives and goal-directed behaviors. Blockers, on the other hand, are those "assumptions" and "forces" in us that obstruct and impede by screening out, or standing in the way, of making change—even when we are consciously or rationally determined or committed to making an important personal change.

Drivers and blockers are powerful forces, yet previous research has largely focused on the role of either drivers *or* blockers, not integrating the two to consider that the same factor can be both a driver *and* a blocker for different people and in different contexts. Our research makes that connection and integration, employing a systems psychodynamic perspective and drawing upon well-established conceptual frameworks (such as Intentional Change Theory and positive psychology).

In particular, we acknowledge that the most important foundation for our research is the work of Robert Kegan and Lisa Lahey (2001a, 2009), whose groundbreaking research on understanding "immunity to change" and "competing commitments" exemplifies a deep understanding of potential blockers in leaders' change efforts. Their work has made an extremely significant contribution to leadership development research, practice and coaching during the past decade and half, and will continue to do so.

## What Is This Book About?

Our book is designed to encapsulate and synthesize the relevant academic literature relating to drivers and blockers; share our own research including field research examples; and provide leadership development scholars and practitioners (such as leadership faculty, coaches and consultants) with concrete approaches and practical material to help explore drivers and blockers. Throughout the book, we show more than 40 examples of drivers and blockers from our field research—including four complete mini case studies—to illuminate the concepts. There is also a copy of our "Drivers and Blockers Exploration Tool" for use or adaptation. We have used that surfacing tool and exploration method with more than 2000 global executives in the past five years.

Throughout the book, we argue that allowing a person to explore both the conscious and unconscious sources and attributes of their drivers and blockers deepens awareness, creates profound insights and increases the chances that meaningful change can occur in the leader's development. We also note the complementarity of the concept of exploring drivers and blockers to a wide range of leadership development approaches including adaptive leadership and personalization, as well as to emotional intelligence. The book also highlights that exploring drivers and blockers in and of itself does not constitute integrated leadership development—rather, it is aimed at increasing profound self-awareness. To be meaningful and actionable, exploring drivers and blockers should be part of a well-designed and integrated leadership development approach that includes feedback, reflection, practice, coaching/mentoring and a support system—all designed to help an individual develop themselves and achieve their desired transformational change over time.

## Acknowledgments and Information

This book progressively developed in its research and writing across the period 2013–2018. The work began when we were all involved at INSEAD—the Business School for the World. We acknowledge the significant assistance in review of the ideas and concepts in this book by a range of current and former INSEAD faculty, including Professors Herminia Ibarra, Eric Uhlmann, Schon Beechler and Narayan Pant.

We also express our gratitude for the review assistance given by Professor Tatiana Bachkirova of Oxford Brookes University (whose work on developmental coaching is extensively cited in our work) and Professor Elizabeth A. More (of the Australian Institute of Management).

During our working time on the book, we were able to provide an earlier draft of our work for reference to Dr. Lisa Lahey of the Harvard Graduate School of Education (whose work on *Immunity to Change* with Robert Kegan is one of the main academic foundations for our work).

Very importantly, we are extremely appreciative of the feedback on exploring drivers and blockers we received from so many INSEAD and other executive program participants and their dedicated coaches (such as Els Valk and Kavitha Iyer—the INSEAD Advanced Management Program coaching directors) as they worked with the concept of drivers and blockers. Program participant and coach feedback contributed strongly to our research. We also acknowledge the numerous examples of exploring drivers and blockers drawn from participants in our programs and coaching work that we have cited throughout the book as anonymized examples.

We acknowledge the permission from British poet William Ayot to reprint one of his poems as a final reflection in the book. We are also thankful for the assistance of Dr. Archana Das Goveravaram at INSEAD, with some of the specialist research editorial work. We are grateful for the editorial work and support of Karthiga Ramu at Springer Nature; as well as to the editorial leaders and staff, including Vishal Daryanomel, the editor, Political Sciences and Business/Economics for Palgrave Macmillan at Springer Nature, who encouraged us in this project and saw it through to completion.

The drivers and blockers information in the book and its exploration tool are presented for reference and use by scholars and practitioners in the field of leadership development, including faculty, coaches and training consultants. We are providing permission for anyone interested in using the tool to do so (see Sect. 10.7). We recognize that our work covers a wide range of research and literature sources—and there are active scholarly debates in many of the areas we raise. So, comments and insights from scholars and practitioners on using the book's concepts and exploration tool will be warmly welcomed—as we will be continuing our work (application and research) on drivers and blockers well into the future. We have all found that exploring drivers and blockers together has led to profound and invaluable insights for leaders trying to create an actionable agenda of transformational change in their leadership development.

| | |
|---|---:|
| Pebble Bay, Singapore | Ian C. Woodward |
| Liverpool, UK | Samah Shaffakat |
| Fontainebleau, France | Vincent H. Believesé |
| November 2018 | |

For information: "Drivers and Blockers Exploration Tool". Access to the tool questions and methodology is found in Sect. 10.8. It is also available with information about the Drivers and Blockers concepts at: www.driversandblockers.com.

## References

Kegan, R., & Lahey, L. (2001a). The real reason people won't change. *Harvard Business Review, 79*(10), 85–92.

Kegan, R., & Lahey, L. (2009). *Immunity to change: How to overcome it and unlock the potential in yourself and in your organization.* Boston: Harvard Business Press.

# Contents

1 **Introduction**     1
   1.1   *What Are Drivers and Blockers?*     3
   1.2   *Overview of the Chapters*     4

2 **Profound Self-Awareness and the Need to Explore Drivers and Blockers**     9
   2.1   *Adult Mind Development Stages and the "Immunity to Change" Process*     13
       2.1.1   Adult Mind Development and Stages     14
       2.1.2   The "Immunity to Change" Process     17

3 **Exploring the Reservoirs of Drivers and Blockers: Conscious and Unconscious Selves**     21
   3.1   *The Role of Conscious and Unconscious Mind, Mini-selves and Possible-Selves*     22
   3.2   *The Conscious and Unconscious Mind*     22
   3.3   *Ego and Mini-selves*     25
   3.4   *Possible-Selves and Identity*     27

## xii CONTENTS

**4 Exploring the Reservoirs of Drivers and Blockers (Conscious and Unconscious): Worldviews and Emotions** — 31
  4.1 Worldviews — 31
  4.2 Emotions — 34
    4.2.1 Emotions in Our Lives — 35
    4.2.2 Emotions and Change — 36

**5 Exploring the Reservoirs of Drivers and Blockers (Conscious and Unconscious): Big Five Personality Traits** — 41
  5.1 Personality Traits: The Five Factor Model — 42

**6 Exploring the Reservoirs of Drivers and Blockers (Conscious and Unconscious): Other Personality Traits and Characteristics** — 51
  6.1 Self-Esteem — 51
  6.2 Locus of Control — 54
  6.3 Self-Efficacy — 55
  6.4 Positive and Negative Affectivity — 57
  6.5 Risk Aversion — 58
  6.6 Tolerance for Ambiguity — 59
  6.7 Other Potential Areas Related to Drivers and Blockers — 60

**7 Exploring the Reservoirs of Drivers and Blockers (Conscious and Unconscious): Values and Motivators** — 63
  7.1 Values — 63
  7.2 Extrinsic and Intrinsic Motivators — 65
  7.3 Summary of the Reservoirs and Sources of Drivers and Blockers — 69

**8 Uncovering, Understanding, Unleashing, Overcoming: Exploring Drivers and Blockers in Leadership Development Practice** — 71
  8.1 The "Drivers and Blockers Exploration Tool" — 71
  8.2 Drivers and Blockers Exploration in Action: The Case of Jennifer — 77
  8.3 Integrating Drivers and Blockers Exploration with Leadership Development — 86

| | | | |
|---|---|---|---|
| 9 | Conclusion and Opportunities for Further Research and Application | | 89 |
| | 9.1 | Afterword: Drivers and Blockers: A Final Reflection | 92 |
| 10 | Appendices | | 95 |
| | 10.1 | Appendix 1: List of Participant Field Research Examples Demonstrating Drivers and Blockers | 95 |
| | 10.2 | Appendix 2: "Orders of Mind" (Adapted from Kegan, 1994 and Additional Sources as Cited) | 100 |
| | 10.3 | Appendix 3: Overcoming Immunity to Change—Kegan and Lahey's (2009) Four Column "Immunity Map"—Information Overview | 102 |
| | 10.4 | Appendix 4: System 1 and System 2—Automatic and Controlled Mind | 105 |
| | 10.5 | Appendix 5: Comparing Five Factor NEO-P (Big Five) with MBTI | 105 |
| | 10.6 | Appendix 6: Summary Description of Various Reservoirs and Sources of Drivers and Blockers | 107 |
| | 10.7 | Appendix 7: Drivers and Blockers Exploration Tool for Use and Adaptation | 113 |
| | 10.8 | Appendix 8: Drivers and Blockers Exploration Tool—Mini Case Study Full Research Examples | 117 |
| | | 10.8.1 Example A: Stefanie—Female—Chief Operating Officer, Energy Company | 117 |
| | | 10.8.2 Example B: Markus—Male—Chief Executive Officer, Regional Consumer Retail Company | 124 |
| | | 10.8.3 Example C: John—Male—Chief Operating Officer, Transport Company | 130 |
| | 10.9 | Appendix 9: Potential Relationship of Exploring Drivers and Blockers with a Selection of Leadership and Development Theories, Models, Frames and Approaches | 134 |

References 139

Author Index 159

Subject Index 161

# List of Figures

| | | |
|---|---|---|
| Fig. 2.1 | Intentional change theory process. (Adapted from Boyatzis (2006)) | 11 |
| Fig. 7.1 | Motivation matrix. (Derived and adapted from Herzberg (1959), Ryan & Deci (2000) and Taylor (2012)) | 67 |
| Fig. 7.2 | Reservoir: conscious and unconscious sources of drivers and blockers | 70 |
| Fig. 8.1 | Drivers and blockers exploration tool overview (2018). (Published with kind permission of the authors © I.C. Woodward, S. Shaffakat and V.H. Dominé (2018). All Rights Reserved. Section 10.7 provides the full tool, its steps and its questions) | 73 |
| Fig. 8.2 | Insightfully aware leadership development framework (2017). (Published with kind permission of the author © I.C. Woodward (2017). All Rights Reserved) | 87 |
| Fig. 10.1 | Drivers and blockers exploration tool (2018 version) (The "Drivers and Blockers Exploration Tool" (2018) is published with kind permission of the authors © I.C. Woodward, S. Shaffakat and V.H. Dominé (2018). All Rights Reserved. The authors also provide that this tool may be copied or disseminated with source attribution, citation and acknowledgement for legitimate use by leadership development researchers and practitioners) | 113 |

# List of Tables

Table 5.1  Big Five personality traits—drivers and blockers examples from our research  43

Table 8.1  Leadership development application example of the drivers and blockers exploration process Mini case example—Jennifer—female—chief financial officer, Specialist Financial Services Firm Development objective explored: lack of active listening with impatience in interactions with others  78

# CHAPTER 1

# Introduction

*Until you make the unconscious conscious, it will direct your life and you will call it fate.*
*Carl Gustav Jung*

Despite good intentions, prioritizing and promising to change,[1] leaders often fail to achieve their personal or professional development objectives, and the changes they desire. Drawing upon academic research, executive development practices and our field research, we advocate an approach to deepen self-awareness, combined with a more integrated development process, that together offer a better chance of accomplishing the development objectives leaders set for themselves. Like other scholars (e.g. Allen & Hartman, 2008; Collingwood, 2001; Hall, 2004; Mayo, Kakarika, Pastor, & Brutus, 2012; Petriglieri, Wood, & Petriglieri, 2011; Yammarino & Atwater, 1993), we see self-awareness as the critical underpinning of effective leadership development.

We argue that profound levels of self-awareness (part of what might be called a leader's "insightful awareness" of self, others, context and

---

[1] Change here refers to any change which is "adaptive" (Heifetz et al., 2009) and involves "the challenge of developing the whole person" (Boyatzis et al., 2002, p. 151) at an intrapersonal level. We note that there is also an extensive literature on organizational change and resistance that is neither the focus of our research studies nor the findings presented in this book.

purpose[2]) (Woodward & Shaffakat, 2016) can be achieved when leaders understand the influence of conscious and unconscious forces that could promote or impede their efforts to change. It is the psychodynamic approach that most consistently emphasizes the role of these forces as major hurdles to an individual's development (Lee, 2010). Our research reviews these different psychological forces—which we call ***drivers*** and ***blockers***—in depth. We promote a leadership development approach that includes *exploring* and *understanding* drivers and blockers to deepen leaders' self-awareness and help them take actions for change. Insights from this deeper level of self-awareness are then integrated into the overall development activities platform for that leader, and supported by other development initiatives such as reflection, coaching, feedback and a change support system.

Derived from our literature review and field research, we also provide a tool developed for exploring drivers and blockers designed to help leaders (and development practitioners) uncover and turn these to advantage. We found that the "Drivers and Blockers Exploration Tool" is an effective diagnostic tool involving a surfacing and discovery process for leaders. The tool helps them seek insights for change or transformation as part of a scenario-building approach and assists them to envision a better future, recasting their situation in a positive light by overcoming potential blockers. By putting a positive spin on their situation, leaders can leverage their drivers to their advantage. Likewise, the tool helps leaders envision situations where blockers can be used as opportunities—turning them into drivers (transforming weaknesses into strengths), as well as avoiding situations where drivers become counterproductive blockers.

---

[2] For further information on the construct of "insightfully aware leaders" and "insightful awareness", readers can access some online content from Professor Ian C. Woodward at:

- https://knowledge.insead.edu/blog/insead-blog/leadership-is-a-journey-not-a-destination-7581
- https://knowledge.insead.edu/blog/insead-blog/the-three-altitudes-of-leadership-7541
- TEDx Talk on the "Altitudes of Leadership": https://www.youtube.com/watch?v=tEGcPExBl_8

## 1.1   What Are Drivers and Blockers?

Drivers are those "assumptions" and "forces" in individuals that create and power activity and give impetus and desire to their actions. These assumptions and forces initiate, guide and sustain people's objectives and goal-directed behaviors. Blockers, on the other hand, are those assumptions and forces in people that obstruct making a change by screening out, or standing in the way of change, even when individuals are consciously or rationally determined to make a change. So, in making any change in ourselves, we are waging an unknown war—essentially a competition between our different conscious and unconscious facets—and this conflict presents both a dilemma and an opportunity for an individual's development.

We note that previous research in this field has largely focused on exploring the role of either the drivers *or* blockers but has paid limited attention to how the same factors can act as both drivers and blockers, which we address in our research. Following Aspinwall & Staudinger (2003), we believe that "…a psychology of human strengths should not be the study of how negative experience [or factors*] may be avoided or ignored, but rather how positive and negative experience [or factors*] may be inter-related" (pp. 14–15)—hence leading us to explore the combination of exploring drivers and blockers.

This combination of looking at both the positive and negative factors or drivers and blockers is also hinted at in the work on executive derailment by McCall (2009) where he argues that "people can and do change in profound ways, even to the point of rewiring the brain, and therefore can develop new strengths as well as correct perceived weaknesses" (p. 44). McCall (2009) is also critical of the assumption that "a strength is a strength is a strength" (p. 44) and that weaknesses can be ignored because an individual's strength is adequate enough to compensate for his or her shortcomings, or because an individual can steer clear of situations where his or her dark side can lead to serious problems. With a change in situation or context, individuals may require different strengths to sustain success. In addition, strengths can be overexploited and used ineffectively in situations which don't require them, or they can turn into flaws in situations that need different strengths (McCall, 2009). The same holds true for drivers, as well as for blockers that can disguise themselves as drivers.

These drivers and blockers and their underlying assumptions and forces arise from different factors (which we call reservoirs or sources), such as worldviews, emotions, personality traits and dispositional variables, as well as values and motivators which shape and are shaped by our experiences. We argue that allowing a person to explore both the conscious and unconscious sides and attributes of these drivers and blockers deepens awareness, creates profound insights and increases the chances that meaningful change can occur.

## 1.2 Overview of the Chapters

In Chap. 2, we address the relationship of self-awareness to leadership development, and the interrelationship of drivers and blockers. Using a systems psychodynamic approach, we also build upon different pedagogical and psychological approaches such as Boyatzis's (2006) "Intentional Change Theory", "Positive Psychology and Positive Leadership" (Diener, 2000; Peterson, 2000; Seligman, 1998a, 1998b; Snyder, 2000), Bachkirova's (2011) "developmental coaching" as well as Kegan (1994) and Kegan & Lahey's (2001a) work on "adult mind development stages" and the "immunity to change" process, respectively. Kegan and Lahey's work provides the largest foundation for grounding our work on drivers and blockers.

Across Chaps. 3, 4, 5, 6, and 7, we then present our literature review of the reservoirs and sources of conscious and unconscious drivers and blockers, which informs and underpins the "Drivers and Blockers Exploration Tool". In this review, we also present relevant and directly related examples from our own research and field work[3] to demonstrate the efficacy of the concept of exploring different drivers and blockers such as mini-selves, possible-selves, worldviews, emotions, the Big Five personality traits, dispositional variables, values, and extrinsic and intrinsic motivators. Understanding there are different kinds of drivers and blockers is a first step in making decisions on one's personal developmental objective.

Exploring the drivers and blockers allows the leader to examine their assumptions, forces and whether possible change outcomes would meet

[3] Between 2013 and 2018, as part of our field research, we included aspects of exploring drivers, blockers or both, in different leadership development programs and coaching or training activities covering more than 2000 executive and senior executive level leaders. All the examples used in this book are drawn from this field research. To maintain confidentiality, the real names of the participants have not been used—and other information has been highly anonymized and disguised. All of our driver and blocker examples are listed in a cross-referenced summary table in Sect. 10.1.

personal blocking resistance or experience personal drive support. It promotes introspection about the ways an individual's intrapersonal and idiosyncratic aspects impact their approach toward change and development. The primary purpose of the exploration is to increase profound self-awareness and enable people to overcome their personal barriers, tap into personal drivers and bring about the required transformation as part of an integrated leadership development process.

In Chap. 8, we present the "Drivers and Blockers Exploration Tool" based on our literature review and our leadership development research, practice and experience. The tool uses a progressive surfacing method that discovers and places these forces at the center of enabling change, by drawing on the psychodynamic approach. It is based on increasing awareness of the structure and nature of different assumptions and forces (i.e. drivers and blockers) that foster or limit the way someone views themselves, and the context, thereby reconstructing this structure to allow for a more complete and comprehensive inclusion of experiences and acting on these new insights. The "Drivers and Blockers Exploration Tool", in particular blockers exploration, is an extension of Kegan & Lahey's (2009) *four-column exercise* on *immunity to change* and Boyatzis's (2006) *Intentional Change Theory,* and incorporates further concepts from the range of integrated leadership development approaches cited throughout the book, together with the outcomes of our field research. Numerous examples are shown throughout the book of those undertaking the drivers and blockers exploration exercise (four full examples are provided as mini case studies in Chap. 8 and Sect. 10.8).

Exploring drivers and blockers in and of itself does not constitute integrated leadership development. Rather, it is aimed at increasing profound self-awareness. To be meaningful, and actionable, such exploration should be part of a well-designed leadership development approach that includes feedback, reflection, practice and a support system—all designed to help an individual progressively develop themselves and achieve transformational change. In this regard, we also give the example of an *"Insightfully Aware Leadership Development Framework"* that incorporates the exploration of drivers and blockers within an integrated leadership development approach.

Chapter 9 posits opportunities for additional research and pedagogical deployment in leadership development, as well as our conclusions. Appendices are also provided to amplify relevant information and concepts covered in the book.

Our work contributes to the literature in various ways. First, it adds to our understanding of the intrapersonal facet of leadership development, which is considered crucial in conceptual scholarship (Ibarra & Petriglieri, 2010; Mayo et al., 2012; Petriglieri et al., 2011; Shamir & Eilam, 2005), yet has received less attention in research. Second, literature on the development of self-awareness of leadership competencies is scant (Mayo et al., 2012). Recognizing how various drivers and blockers influence an individual's approach toward change and development may suggest ways to increase self-awareness and accelerate personal leadership growth. For example, readers with interests in areas such as personality or motivation may find our research examples relating drivers and blockers to the Big Five personality characteristics as well as values, extrinsic and intrinsic motivation particularly interesting.

Last, we develop and provide a "Drivers and Blockers Exploration Tool" which we see as offering a dual approach of exploring hidden change blockers and then focusing on possible change drivers. Although we recognize that more research in different contexts is needed to test our work further, we advocate that leadership development programs and coaching interventions which encourage profound self-awareness may change potential blockers held by many executives into drivers that promote personal learning and development. Throughout the book, we connect our work to leadership transformation efforts, and interrelate exploring drivers and blockers to a range of leadership development methods, as well as coaching approaches and tools.

To set the scene, and bring the drivers and blockers concept into focus, we will share one example of a senior executive leader, named Olivia,[4] who undertook the exploration of drivers and blockers as part of her leadership development work in 2017.

Olivia heads the marketing function in a global cosmetic company. She is extremely passionate and knowledgeable about her company and the trends in the personal care industry, in general. Although she holds a strong track record in her field, she is known to overdominate conversations within the corporate leadership team. She mentions, "I seem to always take up a lot of airtime". This view was also echoed in some of the feedback she received from her peers: "Even though you think you are providing oxygen and energy to the discussion, what you are actually doing is crowding everybody else out". As part of a major leadership development program, Olivia highlighted this issue as her most important leadership development objective.

[4] An example from our research (see Sect. 10.1, Example 42).

She had previously, and unsuccessfully, tried to constrain herself but found it very frustrating. However, after exploring her drivers and blockers, a clearer pathway to change emerged, and she became much more self-aware. She described her behaviors as "always talking first; always talking last; interrupting people; and sometimes even suddenly standing up when she got over excited about an idea".

Olivia is a strong extrovert, the trait which makes her communication approach expressive and visual. While displaying confidence, she describes herself "as somewhat of an insecure overachiever", which she believes is marked by "lot of self-doubt and fairly low self-esteem". She holds the belief that "if you want to get ahead and make your mark, you must always be heard". All these factors are acting as blockers to her change effort. After becoming aware of these factors, she decides it is time to confront and overcome these.

Olivia holds very strong values related to collaboration and teaming. In addition, she is personally motivated by learning. By thinking more deeply about these characteristics, she is determined to increase her own level of listening, making sure others get heard first and reducing her "airtime". To help with it, she has asked two of her colleagues to act in the moment in meetings with her—signaling if her "airtime" is getting too long or loud (which she described as receiving a "yellow card"). These new behaviors she reasons would make the collaboration better—and the listening could be an act of learning. Furthermore, she has a high level of conscientiousness in her personality profile. She cares about doing an outstanding job and contributing to the company and its future. As such, she believes that if she's more engaging with other business area leaders, then she would be working toward achieving collaborative business outcomes across the whole company.

By surfacing these positive attributes, she taps into these as drivers to support her change efforts. After thinking about her drivers and blockers, she decides to also build her change support system. To help with that, she decides to get an experienced mentor, who in comparison to her is quieter and a better listener and displays collaborative gravitas in their approach to engaging with others. She thinks she needs a role model to reinforce the drivers, and that her mentor could help with it.

At the time of writing, Olivia had received very positive feedback on her "airtime" problem and how much progress she's made. She mentions, "It has also helped my own team seem more collaborative with other divisions. I have been given a couple of yellow cards, but I have not jumped up to talk once this year. Now I need to do more reflection and work on building my sense of confidence and self-comfort".

We hope that the chapters ahead encourage the reader to examine both the "why" and "how" of exploring drivers and blockers, and its potential to assist in deepening self-awareness and support change efforts in leadership development.

CHAPTER 2

# Profound Self-Awareness and the Need to Explore Drivers and Blockers

*When you meet someone better than yourself, turn your thoughts to becoming that person's equal. When you meet someone not as good as you are, look within and examine your own self.*
*Confucius*

Developing self-awareness is a critical and fundamental aspect of leadership development and growth. It is labeled as "leadership's first commandment" (Collingwood, 2001, p. 8). According to Goleman (2004), self-awareness involves an in-depth understanding of one's values, emotions, goals, strengths, weaknesses, needs and drives. Self-awareness is fundamental to the concept of "insightful awareness", which includes a profound understanding of one's "strengths, weaknesses, drivers and blockers". Personal self-exploration to make ourselves more aware can help us become more open to change. Indeed, the development "process of *personalization*" itself strengthens ability in self-awareness, where learning "helps to integrate past, present, and future; cognitive and emotional; personal and professional aspects of the individual's life" (Petriglieri et al., 2011, p. 445). We argue that exploring drivers and blockers (such as using the surfacing tool we propose) constitutes part of the personalization process, one that is set in the context or situation and is related to specific development objectives.

The drivers and blockers exploration approach builds on a systems psychodynamic perspective (French & Vince, 1999; Petriglieri & Stein, 2012), which addresses the organizational and social phenomenon by combining open systems and psychodynamic theories (Menzies, 1960; Miller & Rice, 1967) and is considered very effective for studying "change journeys" of individuals (Woodman & Dewett, 2004). Such a perspective is based on the assumption that the self contains contradictory and diverse elements, and attempts to explain how the tensions between these selves are understood and managed, socially as well as intrapsychically (Gabriel, 1999). As such, it is well suited to look deeply into the different elements of personal development. By focusing on conscious and unconscious factors, this approach can help explain aspects of individual change problems which otherwise might have been neglected. The conscious realization of these factors helps an individual to avoid misleading himself or herself into an image of who they are "that feeds on itself, becomes self-perpetuating, and eventually may become dysfunctional" (Goleman, 1985) as seen in Boyatzis (2006, p. 614).

For most people, understanding these elements and becoming comfortable including them as part of one's self-will should represent significant personal discovery and development. This notion is shared by Boyatzis & McKee (2006), who believe that, "part of the challenge of creating and sustaining excellent leadership is to recognize, manage, and even direct one's own process of learning and change". Managing one's own development, on the other hand, requires increasing self-awareness and making sound choices about the courses of action needed to improve efficacy as well as to accomplish the changes desired. Having worked with large numbers of leaders, we see that there are significant consequences for individuals, teams and organizations, where leaders do not possess sufficient self-awareness. These unaware leaders usually have a surplus of blind spots that are negatively affecting their interactions and behaviors. Consequently, they can wreak havoc, inflict damage and demoralize others. Demotivated and fearful workforces with low productivity and engagement are the result. This is one reason that accelerating and deepening self-awareness by exploring drivers and blockers is so important to help achieve change.

According to Boyatzis's (2006) "Intentional Change Theory" (ICT), the change process comprises a series of "discoveries", which work as a continuous cycle in bringing about sustainable and long-lasting change in individuals. This series of steps includes an understanding of one's "ideal self",[1] that is, what one wants to be; the "real self"[2] and how it stands next to one's "ideal self", leading to an evaluation of one's strengths and weaknesses; a learning and development agenda; testing out and engaging one's new behaviors, perceptions and actions; and enduring and resonant relationships that help one to live, analyze and interpret each "discovery" as it happens. Critical to all these steps is the capacity to increase awareness, receive feedback and support, as well as apply continuous learning from experience. This is graphically represented below by adding in the exploration of drivers and blockers to the ICT frame (see Fig. 2.1).

Consistent with the Boyatzis (2006) approach, we contend that this interlinking sequence of "discoveries", which can lead to sustainable change in individuals, involves developing insightful awareness, which helps a person identify and understand the different "forces" in operation

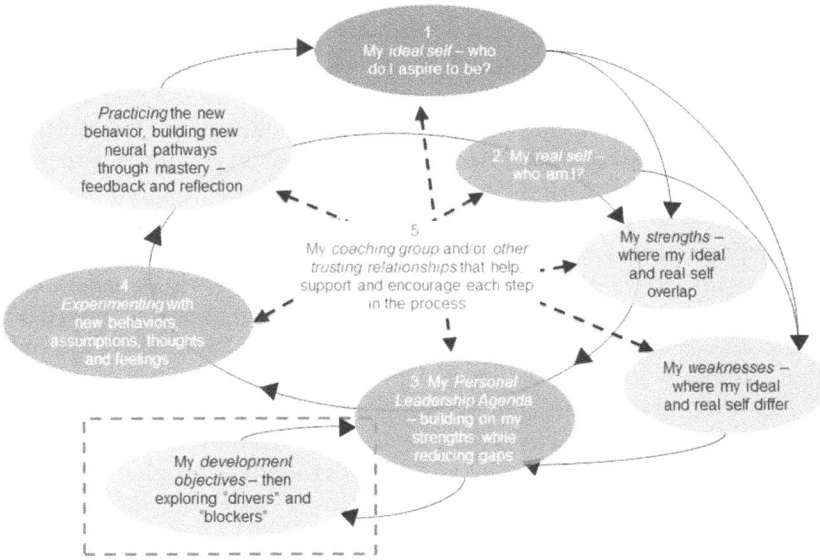

**Fig. 2.1** Intentional change theory process. (Adapted from Boyatzis (2006))

[1] This refers to the self we want to be. It is the psychological element of self, which is to some extent conscious and to some extent unconscious and is different for different individuals (Boyatzis & Akrivou, 2006).
[2] An individual's actual behavior (Boyatzis & Akrivou, 2006).

in themselves. In other words, it involves ***uncovering and understanding*** the "assumptions" and "forces" which influence or act as the drivers and blockers; ***overcoming*** the blockers, which might create conflict, competition and change incoherence; and ***unleashing*** the drivers to support the changes desired.

The idea of exploring ***both*** drivers and blockers and not just blockers also draws from the field of positive psychology, which follows that, "what is good about life is as genuine as what is bad and therefore deserves equal attention" (Peterson & Seligman, 2004, p. 4). The movement is led by Seligman (1998a, 1998b) and other psychologists (e.g. Ed Diener (2000), Christopher Peterson (2000) and Rick Snyder (2000)), who argue for a need to focus on strengths and adaptability in people, rather than continuing on the path of looking into and fixing negatives or weaknesses. Scholars (e.g. Luthans, 2002) contend that in organizational behavior studies, negatives (such as resistance, burnout and stress) have received much more attention than positives.

Positive psychology, although more researched than so-called feel-good perspectives (promoted in popular media), has received criticism from a number of scholars (e.g. Held, 2004; Krippner, Pitchford, & Davies, 2012). For example, Barbara Held (2004) maintains that the theory is self-contradictory in its presentation and construction. For her, some scholars of the positive psychology movement disregard the notions or perspectives that oppose the positive psychology's dominant message, being *negativity about negativity itself* and *negativity about the wrong kind of positivity* (p. 9). Positive psychology has also been criticized for its failure to adequately identify the vital roles of "*negative*" emotions (Krippner et al., 2012).

However, like Aspinwall & Staudinger (2003), we believe that "a psychology of human strengths should not be the study of how negative experience [or factors*] may be avoided or ignored, but rather how positive and negative experience [or factors*] may be inter-related" (pp. 14–15)—hence the combination of exploring drivers *and* blockers. Since drivers are beneficial, individuals can develop as many of them as they are able; however, not all drivers might serve equally well. Sometimes drivers can be over-used or become peripheral; drivers in combination with some blockers may be harmless in some situations and detrimental in others. Some blockers may also be drivers, not easy to assess or to change; however, the risk here is that they may be seen as the very drivers that are suggested for people to draw on in their everyday work.

Identifying both drivers and blockers and their combinations can help an individual to understand the complex interactions between these, as well as how these are relative and situationally determined. This is also hinted at in the work of McCall (2009) on executive derailment, in which he questions the notion that strengths are always strengths or that weaknesses can be ignored. McCall (2009) sees people as a farrago of strengths and weaknesses, and knowing and understanding their strengths and weaknesses necessitates studying combinations of both of these in specific situations.

For example, the "Drivers and Blockers Exploration Tool", in particular, acts as a structured surfacing method for people to engage in becoming aware of the forces sitting behind strengths and weaknesses. This constitutes a step toward emancipation—the significance of changing an individual's structure of assumptions and forces that contribute to his or her way of thinking and interpreting. Bringing about this "insightful awareness" contributes to thinking and practice in leadership development by: increasing understanding of why changing behavior is not a simple process; uncovering the reasons as to why accomplishing the desired change does not follow the path that one might prefer and opening the mind to positive drivers to support the change desired.

Profound self-awareness is even more relevant for leaders attempting to navigate the modern world and create sense and meaning. This so-called D-VUCAD[3] world of disruption, volatility, uncertainty, complexity, ambiguity and diversity presents challenges and opportunities for business and for personal, team and talent development, as well as for the need to develop new mindsets, capabilities and leadership approaches or seek innovation or lead major change. For example, see Beechler and Woodward (2009); Woodward and Shaffakat (2017).

## 2.1 Adult Mind Development Stages and the "Immunity to Change" Process

Although there are a number of adult development theories proposed in the literature, such as by Kegan (1982), Loevinger (1976, 1987) and Torbert (1991), to give a reasonable focus for our research work, we concentrated on Kegan's (1982) adult mind development theory, which

---

[3] "D-VUCAD" as a construct of contemporary business context is described in: https://knowledge.insead.edu/blog/insead-blog/leadership-is-a-journey-not-a-destination-7581

provides a strong foundation for arguments we propose later in the book. We also provide a description of Kegan & Lahey's (2001a) "immunity to change" process, which built on these authors' work on adult mind development. The emphasis here is on exploring the inner and intrinsic self, which paradoxically is a place of both great innovation and those dark and susceptible areas of self, which people prefer not to expose (Chuck 2007).

Predicated on Ronald Heifetz's theory that elucidates the important distinction between "technical[4]" and "adaptive[5]" problems, Kegan & Lahey (2009) contend that certain individual change problems are "adaptive" in nature and necessitate developing bigger or transforming mindsets. In other words, we have to adapt so as to learn how to solve complex change challenges. Kegan and Lahey developed a process that evolved from merely "diagnosing" immunities to change to "overcoming" immunities to change, thereby fulfilling both objectives simultaneously (p. xii). The "immunity to change" process helps in exposing "hidden" commitments and the assumptions behind them. This understanding then enhances mental complexity, transforming mindsets from subject to object. Furthermore, the ability to change the individual's mindset and move it to a more effective and more advanced level is as a critical strength to address difficult adaptive problems (Kegan & Lahey, 2009).

### 2.1.1 Adult Mind Development and Stages

The idea behind transformation or knowing is epistemological change, not just change in the behavioral pattern (Kegan, 2000). In other words, what someone does is not to just construct or change their meanings but rather change the very *form* of the meaning-making system, that is, their epistemologies.[6]

---

[4] Technical problems are the problems that are very mechanical and require quick and easy fixes (Heifetz, 1994).

[5] Adaptive problems, on the other hand, have no straightforward solution or quick fixes available. These problems necessitate a transformation in beliefs, ideologies, values and ways of working (Heifetz, 1994).

[6] The concept of meaning-making is different to that of sense-making (Weick, 1995) which is seen as more "automatic and immediate" (van den Heuvel, Demerouti, Schreurs, Bakker, & Schaufeli, 2009, p. 511). van den Heuvel et al. (2009) further see meaning-making as a "psychological process of in-depth, internal exploration of an issue of concern" (p. 511).

Kegan's "meaning-forming/making" framework sets forth five qualitatively different levels or "orders of mind" after early childhood (Kegan, 1982, 1994). These "orders of mind" are principles for the *organization* of an individual's thinking, emotions and relating to others rather than the *content* of an individual's thinking, emotions and relating to others (Kegan, 1994). Each level or order of mind involves "looking at" (object) a paradigm, which in the previous level one could only manage to "look through" (subject), that is, the subject/object relation is core to these levels or orders. In other words, it means we can have a more objective view when we advance to high orders, and as such are not trapped in our own "frame".

Drath (1990) explains the role of subject and object through the example of "cultural blindness":

> We see with our culture-bound norms and expectations, accept them as given, and cannot examine them for what they are – that is, we cannot see through them. Our cultural heritage is something we are, not something we have. The culture holds us; we are embedded in it and cannot rise above it. A cognitive development shift, however, is possible when we become aware of culturally determined differences and the distance they create from others. Such understanding could make cultural influences an Object, opening up new ways of seeing ourselves and of relating to others. (1990, p. 48)

The first two orders of mind, that is, "impulsive mind" and "instrumental mind", relate to the significant developments that take place during childhood and as such will not be discussed here. The majority of adults engage in "meaning-making" between the third level (i.e. "socialized mind") and the fourth (i.e. "self-authoring mind"), and only a small fraction of adults advance to the fifth level (i.e. "self-transforming mind") (Kegan, 1994; Torbert et al., 2004). A detailed overview of these three adult higher "orders of mind" (socialized mind, self-authoring mind and self-transforming mind) is provided in Sect. 10.2.

Each level of mental complexity in the three "orders of mind" is more sophisticated than the previous level, since it can accomplish the mental activity of the previous level, as well as additional functions. So, the higher level of mental complexity is more advanced and surpasses the lower level in performance (Kegan & Lahey, 2009). For example, in exercising leadership, scholars (e.g. Helsing & Howell, 2014; Kegan, 1994; McAuliffe, 2006; Rooke & Torbert, 1998) argue that leaders, with advanced levels of mental complexity, can better deal with leadership challenges and thus can be more effective. Also, the differences in approach of leaders with some being transactional and some transformational are explained through Kegan's "orders of mind" (McCauley, Drath, Palus, O'Connor, & Baker, 2006). Kuhnert & Lewis (1987) attribute the differences between these two leadership styles to the different "orders of mind". Leaders with these two styles differ in the manner in which they view and construct reality (i.e. leadership issues and challenges).

Transactional leaders, for example, depend on associations predicated on mutual support, expectations, promises and economic exchange with their followers—this aligns with the "socialized mind", where individuals are identified by their relations with others. Transformational leaders, on the other hand, use their personal value system to inspire followers to espouse it. This style of leadership is more in line with the "self-authoring" mind, where the individuals' self-identity stems from their self-determination. These individuals rise above their self-interest for the common organizational objective (Kuhnert & Lewis, 1987).

McCauley et al.'s (2006) work also maintains that leaders at the self-authoring level are more inclined to lead in ways considered effective by contemporary organizations. These leaders are "more likely to delegate, hold people accountable, influence through rewards and expertise (rather than coercive power), look for underlying causes of problems, act as change agents, and be more comfortable with conflict" (McCauley et al., 2006, p. 647). These findings are similar to the findings of a study by Hasegawa (2004) conducted on nine teachers taking on leadership roles.

Furthermore, research by Van Velsor & Drath (2004) on 25 leaders showed that leaders operating at the "socialized mind" level experienced greater difficulties in handling complex challenges at work than the ones operating at "self-authoring" levels. The leaders in this study were challenged "by being in a role that was ill-defined, becoming a member of a more senior group, needing to take a minority position in a group or with a superior, presenting oneself authentically in stressful situations, and facing competing demands from work and home lives" (p. 400).

Scholars (e.g. Eigel, 1998; Kegan & Lahey, 2009; McCauley et al., 2006; Torbert et al., 2004) contend that the current business world requires the workforce, which is currently at the socialized mind level, to be at the self-authoring mind level. Kegan & Lahey (2009), in particular, stress that the times that required managers to keep their performance within given constraints, while applying power through personal attributes to promote one's position and stand firm in the face of opposition, have changed. Research on talent concurs (e.g. Beechler & Woodward, 2009). The current business world requires managers who can transform their organization—its vision, mission and culture—to adapt to or cope with external demands of the D-VUCAD world described earlier.

With these debates as background, Kegan & Lahey (2009) point to the increased demand for mental complexity in work, which has become more complicated. The same is confirmed by data from two big studies by Kegan (1994) and Torbert (1987) on mental complexity distribution levels across adults. This research indicates a huge gap between the existing and the expected levels of people's minds. All in all, studies over time highlight the necessity for "self-authorship" in the application of a range of skills and competencies that are vital for success across different facets of an individual's personal and professional life and impact on his or her ability to lead (Helsing & Howell, 2014).

We argue that exploring specific drivers and blockers in ourselves can play a role in helping leaders advance to higher order levels of self-authoring and self-transforming minds, thereby mitigating the gap between their own mental complexity and the complexity of the world.

### 2.1.2 The "Immunity to Change" Process

Kegan & Lahey (2001b) developed the "immunity to change" discovery process or the four-column "immunity map" (see Sect. 10.3 for additional details) by studying people who genuinely wanted to change but somehow failed to effect the changes they initiated. Their analysis led them to understand and uncover the reasons, often beyond the conscious level, why a change initially committed to fails to accomplish the desired results. These reasons are referred to as "competing commitments" (McAvoy & Butler, 2005) which, along with the related "big assumptions" (which we describe as blockers), guide and direct one's behaviors and actions.

These "big assumptions" are deeply embedded beliefs about the nature of reality and how one recognizes it (Kegan & Lahey, 2001a). These might be rooted in fear and other negative emotions attributed to life experiences. These "big assumptions", as well as the immune system (a metaphor used by Kegan and Lahey), form the elements of one's reality and hinder the process of accomplishing the very change one is committed to make.

The immune system is a complicated, stable arrangement, prudently formed for self-protection and handling fears and insecurities. The change in "beliefs" or "assumptions" on which this system stands leads the immune system to perceive the state as a threat, triggering resistance behaviors (Kegan & Lahey, 2009). Bowe, Lahey, Armstrong, & Kegan (2003) believe that, "like many New Year's resolutions, sincere intent to change may be short lived and followed by a discouraging return to old behaviors" (p. 715). Similarly, Banerjee (2003, p. 74) defines "competing commitments" as "self-defeating behavior", which is hidden and opposes the change process.

As an exemplar of this, consider Lorenz,[7] a business head in the automotive industry we worked with, who was committed to empower his team members. During the drivers and blockers exploration exercise, he admitted that he does not trust people, which he saw as a main blocker preventing him from empowering his team members. He held the assumption that only by keeping direct control over crucial tasks would he be able to ensure high quality delivery, which he was "known for" and which had contributed to his success to date. By taking him through the exploration of drivers, Lorenz was also able to reconnect to another strong value of his, which was autonomy. During his early years, his superiors constantly pushed him out of his comfort zone and provided him with opportunities to take ownership and responsibility for things he knew little about. This had contributed to his success and personal growth. The awareness of that driver in him made him realize that he would want to be a leader who promotes the same kind of growth environment in his organization and for his people. This deeper awareness of the drivers and blockers which were impacting his change objective created the possibility for him to experiment with empowering his team and eventually integrating the element of "trusting and developing others" in his leadership style. His assumption that only tight control would ensure quality results was proven wrong through tangible and courageous practice of this new behavior.

The notion of transformative change stems from adult development and learning theory (discussed above) which explains the variations and development patterns in people's (adults) construction and perception of themselves and their realities (Basseches, 1984; Kegan, 1982; Kelly, 1955). The process of evaluating people's cognitive mechanisms affects an advancement to an improved thinking and reasoning and increased cogni-

---

[7] An example from our research (see Sect. 10.1, Example 1).

tive complexity (Bochman & Kroth, 2010). For a transformative change to take place, it is imperative that the person's "competing commitments" and the related hidden "assumptions" (the blockers) are reconsidered and restated. These become deep insights for change action. This is because our immune system does not just hinder progress on a single goal; it also adheres to our adult mental complexity continuum. This means something in us is not just competing against one goal, one objective, one job; but rather the way of looking at many things, creating a meaning-making lens as if we are stuck at the lower level or orders of mind.

The process of the immunity to change gives people an "outside" as well as "inside" view on the dynamics of adult mind development (Kegan & Lahey, 2009, p. 47). These views can help people to look deeper into their immune system, a mechanism that guards people, or as Kegan & Lahey (2009) describe, "an intelligent force that seeks to protect you and even to save your life" (p. 47). Reflecting upon these concepts of self-protection and intelligence provides people with more detailed knowledge, which tells individuals that development involves the "head and heart" functioning together.

As such, we now traverse many different aspects of the "head and heart" including the conscious and unconscious mind; ego and mini-selves, possible-selves; worldviews; emotions; personality; dispositional variables; values; and extrinsic and intrinsic motivators—these constitute the reservoirs or sources for the assumptions and forces influencing or acting as drivers and blockers in the change process in ourselves. These reservoirs of drivers and blockers are reflected in the "Drivers and Blockers Exploration Tool" questionnaire. Before turning to that model and the tool, the next five chapters cover the research and literature, as well as provide examples about the reservoirs or sources of drivers and blockers.

CHAPTER 3

# Exploring the Reservoirs of Drivers and Blockers: Conscious and Unconscious Selves

*Every extension of knowledge arises from making conscious the unconscious.*
*Friedrich Nietzsche*

The impetus for us to explore drivers and blockers and their sources is to better understand how the human mind works and apply this understanding to the potential to create profound insights about self, others and context. To emphasize again, previous research has largely focused on exploring the role of either the drivers or blockers, but has paid little attention to how the same factors can act as both drivers and blockers.

From a psychodynamic point of view, identifying and examining *both* drivers and blockers helps individuals to understand why bringing about a change in behavior is not a simple process; uncover the reasons as to why accomplishing the desired change does not follow the path that one might prefer; and why achieving change does not take place more often. We place drivers and blockers as sources of change undertaking and change resistance, as motivations and influences behind the goal of changing or not changing behavior and accomplishing or not accomplishing transformation. By uncovering and understanding how these can be employed for one's benefit, one can gain more leverage in overcoming the blockers that impede one's change efforts, and the same time use one's drivers to support and mobilize the desired change.

In this regard, we now address debates around conscious/unconscious mini-selves and, possible-selves to understand their roles as drivers and blockers in a person's change efforts. The other sources of drivers and blockers such as world views; emotions; personality traits; dispositional variables; values and other external and internal motivators will be discussed subsequently in Chaps. 4, 5, 6, and 7 respectively.

## 3.1 The Role of Conscious and Unconscious Mind, Mini-selves and Possible-Selves

Like Kegan (1994), we believe that the concept of mind is not simply confined to cognition (understanding and acquiring knowledge), but also involves an individual's capacity to create and organize meaning. This includes the capacities to prefer, construe and apply—capacities previously linked to the "ego" or the "self". As William Perry said, "Organisms organize… and human organisms organize meaning" (as seen in Kegan 1994, p. 29).

This idea is not limited to cognition, if someone perceives cognition as a thought process, detached from emotions and relating to others. It is about the sense of organization people employ in their cognition, emotion, social-relating and self-relating. Furthermore, we discuss below how the unconscious and innate "forces" contribute to the ways in which individuals interact with reality, altering their needs as well as roles into actions. We also review the concept of "mini-selves" developed by Tatiana Bachkirova (2011) to illustrate the tension between different conscious and unconscious influences when change is attempted, before turning to the discussion on the role of possible-selves and worldviews in influencing people's responses to change.

## 3.2 The Conscious and Unconscious Mind

A number of studies (e.g. Kegan and Lahey, 2009; Olson, 1990; Robbins and Finley, 1998) ascribe change resistance behaviors to unconscious and automatic processes. The concepts of unconscious and automaticity rest on the understanding that some behaviors in people are involuntary; and that the conscious mind has a limited capacity in comparison to unconscious and automatic processes (George, 1956; Norretranders, 1998).

Although the term "unconscious" was introduced in the eighteenth century by Ernst Platner, a German philosopher (Hendrix, 2015), the concept was popularized by Sigmund Freud (1856–1939). Freud argued that the percentage of conscious versus unconscious thoughts in someone's mind varies greatly. According to him, humans are unaware of the reasons as to why they act or behave in certain ways. Freud even believed ego (conscious and realistic dimension) is not completely conscious; however, it works in keeping with the "reality principle", that is, it deals with reality. Furthermore, it mediates between the commands and drives of id (instinctive drives dimension) and super ego (moralistic dimension) and is itself an outcome of an ingrained conflict between conscious and subconscious (Sandler, 2011).

Post-Freud, scholars moving beyond the id and super ego often take a more practical stand to describe a person's unconscious self. Nobel Prize winner Daniel Kahneman (2011), in his book *Thinking Fast and Slow*, differentiates between automatic[1] and controlled processes,[2] where automatic processes are seen as fast, effective and not in the domain of conscious and thereby lacking forethought and consideration, while controlled processes are seen as requiring intentional and deliberate engagement of conscious thought. Like Freud's id and ego, the automatic and controlled processes function in a manner that is complementary, and at times contradictory.

Freudian and post-Freudian psychology provides us with critical knowledge about human nature, thereby resulting in approaches to deal with psychological disorders as well as giving deeper insights into a person with regard to their conflicts and associations. A benefit of Freud's theory is that the job of the unconscious is not neglected anymore, whether in change (Kegan & Lahey, 2009) or coaching (Lee, 2010). It is widely acknowledged now that a person's unconscious and automatic processes that function beyond conscious control frequently moderate attitudes, opinions and judgment processes as well as violence, conformity, obedience, bias and other related behaviors (Ferreira, Garcia-Marques, Sherman,

---

[1] Automatic processes are referred to as System 1 by Kahneman (2011).
[2] Controlled processes are referred to as System 2 by Kahneman (2011).
Kahneman borrows these terms from psychologists Keith Stanovich and Richard West (Kahneman, 2011). Section 10.4 provides a brief summary of System 1 and System 2 characteristics for reference.

& Sherman, 2006; Kahneman, 2003; Kahneman & Frederick, 2002; Kihlstrom, 1999; Tiffany, 1990).

Bachkirova (2011) adapts Haidt's (2006) famous rider and elephant metaphor to explain that the job of the conscious mind as a rider in the functioning of the entire individual is exaggerated. In Bachkirova's version of the metaphor, the rider is like the conscious part of the mind, and the elephant is both the unconscious mind and the rest of a person's organism. Although the rider's role is to engage in thinking, understanding and meaning-making of experiences through linguistic communication and imagination, yet it is the elephant—the rest of the individual—that interacts with the surroundings and responds. One's consciousness—or the rider—functions under the assumption that it has tight control of the entire individual.

In fact, the rider is under an "illusion of control": the conscious mind has much less power over the rest of the organism than it generally believes. Haidt (2006) makes two important points about the independence of the unconscious. First, like an elephant, the unconscious can make its own decisions. If the rider and the elephant come to the edge of a cliff, the rider does not need to tell the elephant to stop. Unlike a car that is always directed by a driver, the elephant will certainly stop on its own without the rider's intervention. Second, the unconscious has its own agenda, and if that agenda conflicts with what the conscious mind wants to achieve, the unconscious will get its way. Just as the rider cannot physically force the elephant to do what it does not want to do, the conscious mind cannot ultimately over-ride the unconscious by sheer force of willpower. However, for Bachkirova (2011), it is normal and unavoidable that individuals experience a sense of conscious ownership over the whole organism. She puts forth a different construct called "mini-selves" (a combination of cerebral and mind processes responsible for an individual's engagement with his or her surroundings which will be discussed later in the chapter).

Understanding the influence that the conscious and unconscious has on people is important for individuals to perceive themselves, the world around them as well as their actions. In particular, knowing the dynamics and functioning of the unconscious is critical for us so as to not get overpowered by impulses that are difficult to comprehend and control, which is also an aim of the psychodynamic approach. Furthermore, the conscious and unconscious house a number of factors such as a person's mini-selves, possible-selves, worldviews, emotions, personality traits and dispositional variables, values and other extrinsic and intrinsic motivators, which operate in different ways, shaping behaviors and acting as drivers and blockers in change efforts.

We believe that the unconscious can hinder a person's efforts in accomplishing a goal with no conscious deliberation needed. The unconscious influences are believed to have a propensity to draw energy away from the change process (Oldham and Kleiner, 1990) and are seen as reasons for inefficiency and resistance at individual and organizational levels (de Board, 1983).

The unconscious, therefore, can act as a driver as well as a blocker in efforts to achieve change objectives. The same holds true for the conscious. For example, a rational decision to make a change in ourselves based on a leadership development agenda and feedback will be driven by the person's consciousness, which can act as a driver here. Through different factors such as mini-selves, possible-selves, worldviews, emotions, personality traits and dispositional variables, values and extrinsic and intrinsic motivators, the unconscious can influence the cognitive mental processes of the conscious.

## 3.3 Ego and Mini-selves

According to Bachkirova (2011, p. 63), an individual's interactions with reality are served by a number of "mini-selves", the majority of which are unconscious and translate the different needs of an individual as well as his/her functions into actions. She calls this web of mini-selves "ego". This term includes a mix of states and processes of the brain and mind that are responsible for the entire individual's involvement with a specific role. "Mini-self" specifically is a pattern of associations between various points of the brain that are activated or inhibited when an individual performs an action (Bachkirova, 2011). These patterns may include a range of factors: memory processes, thinking, meaning-making and so forth (Passmore, Peterson, & Freire, 2012). These may lead to adjustment to intrinsic condition and external environment. Action might not necessarily entail a physical process but rather could be demonstrated through communication or avoiding taking an action (Bachkirova, 2011).

Bachkirova (2011) explains the working of the "mini-selves" through an image proposed by Claxton (1994) where he portrays the brain as a group of octopuses, some of which are awake and might stimulate the ones that are not, through mingling and dancing, thereby causing the individual to act. While they are mingling and dancing, with each contributing and participating to different extents, an individual can engage in various roles.

Bachkirova (2011) calls this group of octopuses "mini-selves". So, when an individual performs various roles, different mini-selves appear at different times and surface continuously throughout our lives. Some of these tend to be simple and some are complicated. These might demonstrate specific kinds of behaviors reflecting the personality characteristics of an individual. This link with the personality has also been suggested in the works of Browning (1980), and Carter (2008).

The notion of "mini-selves", in particular, shares similarities with the notion of "selves" offered by Rita Carter (2008) in her book *Multiplicity*. According to her, we as individuals house a repertoire of different selves or personalities in our head. These selves become apparent and continuously flow through us on an everyday basis; the self which surfaces when we are angry, the self that emerges when we are depressed, the annoyed self, the self as a caring friend and so on. Each of these selves has its own way of functioning (perspective, feelings and ambitions), i.e. the way it manifests itself (Carter, 2008).

Furthermore, there can be times when an individual is conscious of conflict between various "mini-selves" at the same time (Browning, 1980; Passmore et al., 2012). As William James explained in his famous 1890 work on the principles of psychology:

> *I am often confronted by the necessity of standing by one of my empirical selves and relinquishing the rest. Not that I would not. If I could, be... a great athlete and make a million a year, be a wit, a bon-vivant and a lady killer, as well as a philosopher, a philanthropist ... and saint. But the thing is simply impossible. The millionaire's work would run counter to the saint s; the bon-vivant and the philanthropist would trip each other up; the philosopher and the lady killer could not well keep house in the same tenement of clay.* (James, 2007, pp. 309–310)

From one point of view, we can argue that these 'mini-selves' are unconscious, since we are not familiar with the brain processes that relate to our interaction with the world. Yet, we may be aware of the functioning of the entire cycle and identify cognitive, affective and behavioral patterns related to it. We can accept that we do indeed identify this mini-self (Bachkirova, 2011).

As individuals, we need to be aware of the apprehensions or issues of conflicting "selves" or "mini-selves" in bringing about the change or achieving our development objectives (Bachkirova, 2011). We believe that certain selves or mini-selves can act as blockers in an individual's change efforts. These might perform their roles as suits them and may even fulfill their needs, which then conflict with one another. A good example would be of a "powerless" self that responds to stressful situations by making an individual think he/she is helpless and that he/she cannot achieve the tasks assigned to him/her. Such an individual might feel alone, anxious and hopeless, and may give up trying.

However, selves or "mini-selves" can also act as drivers in the change process, if they are complementary or if there is coordination and communication between them. This can be explained through the example of the "resourceful" self that reacts to opportunities by considering itself worthy and capable of performing a task, and the "inquisitive" self that is curious and open when faced with new experiences and change. Both these selves together could generate optimism leading to creativity, purposefulness and thereby dedicated change.

As human beings we could recognize the "selves" or "mini-selves" which act as blockers causing problems and impeding the links between other selves or mini-selves, and work toward making them passive and confine them to the background while putting the selves which are drivers into active roles.

## 3.4 Possible-Selves and Identity

Markus & Nurius (1986) refer to possible-selves as a domain of one's self-knowledge with regard to how one sees one's ability and thinks about one's future. Specifically, they see possible-selves as "cognitive manifestation[s] of enduring goals, aspirations, motives, fears, threats" (p. 158). A person's possible future selves are more than a set of idealized roles or states of existence; they reflect the individual's idiosyncratically significant hopes, fears and thoughts. They are the selves someone wishes to become as positive aspirations (e.g. prosperous self, famous self, highly regarded self) or fear becoming (e.g. incapable self, solitary self, addict-self) (Markus & Nurius, 1986) and can be shaped by their social roles (Goffman, 1959). Erikson (2007) points out that all fears and hopes do not automatically make possible-selves which serve as more than an abstract view of the future and include an experience of "what it would be like if the situation comes true" (p. 350).

Possible-selves encompass a person's self-representations of their past as well as their future. Though distinguishable from their current selves, these are closely linked to them (Markus & Nurius, 1986). Possible-selves are personalized as well as social (Markus & Nurius, 1986; Oyserman, Bybee, & Terry, 2006).

Past selves can also constitute possible-selves in the sense they may influence an individual in the future. The past selves that are transmitted as possible-selves or their components express an individual's fears or worries and the actions that result in these fears and worries (Markus & Nurius, 1986). These selves are a direct outcome of past social comparison, where one's emotions, views, attributes and behaviors have been compared to those of significant others (Markus & Nurius, 1986). For example, a self-conscious possible self may include the view, "I used to be constantly compared to my siblings who were exceptional students". And the disliked self is linked to the unpleasant memory, "I used to get average grades". Development here can be viewed as a process of gaining and then accomplishing or opposing specific possible-selves.

The concept of possible-selves originated in the domain of cognitive research of one's notions and beliefs of oneself—self-concept (e.g. Greenwald, 1988; Greenwald et al., 2002; Greenwald & Pratkanis, 1984; Markus & Wurf, 1987). Possible-selves are viewed as components of the self-concept (e.g. Markus & Ruvolo, 1989; Wurf & Markus, 1991), especially with regard to its focus on the individualized meaning construction. The manner in which self-concept impacts possible-selves is when the likelihood or prospects of possible-selves are influenced by the current existing notions or understanding of one's capacities or shortcomings (Erikson, 2007).

By way of example, consider Takashi,[3] a general manager at a professional services organization, who we recently worked with, and who had a self-concept that involved the view of not being good at team work and people-oriented skills in general, and who, at the same time, also had a focused, positive possible self as being a CEO in the future. The likelihood of realizing this possible self in his case was impacted by the current existing self where he learned about the significance of team work and people-oriented skills in running an organization. As shown in this example,

---

[3] An example from our research (see Sect. 10.1, Example 2).

self-concept can also generate several negative selves as an unsuccessful professional.

Sensitive to circumstances, possible-selves convey novel and incongruent knowledge regarding oneself (Markus & Nurius, 1986), which might occur during change. However, individuals might react to their possible-selves by taking no action, as when these possible-selves continue existing as dreams, or with rejection; or they may include the possible-selves into a modified self-concept (Schouten, 1991). As such, these can serve as "perceptual screens, shaping one's interpretations of, and responses to, unfolding opportunities or constraints" (Ibarra, 2007, p. 9). In other words, these can act as both drivers and blockers in one's change efforts.

Possible-selves serve as a link between self-knowledge and motivation (Markus & Nurius, 1986). A manager who fears that he will not get promoted to the director level is not just carrying a fear of getting stuck in a particular position; rather it goes to a personal level, where that manager tends to have an elaborated possible self that conveys the fear—the failed self, the incompetent self, the cynical self, the self as a professional who is not being trusted by the top management. Negative possible-selves can act as drivers as well as blockers, motivating people to work more toward achieving their objectives; or demotivating them and preventing them from taking steps to achieve their objectives.

As components of one's self-system, possible-selves enable individuals to model essential strategies for achieving their goals (see MacKay, 1981; Markus & Ruvolo, 1989; Richardson, 1967), thereby acting as drivers. Possible-selves help individuals to direct their focus on particular task-specific thoughts and feelings and to direct and coordinate action (Inglehart, Markus, & Brown, 1988). Overall, possible-selves serve as a link between current existing states and the ends (Oyserman & Markus, 1990). Activating a desired possible self may promote positive emotions and the desire to uphold and improve this state. Even when faced with disappointments, such an individual will have access to possible-selves that can be employed to revive positive emotions (Cross & Markus, 1994).

The impact of self, however, is more wide ranging (Cross & Markus, 1994). For example, an individual who has a self-concept as being conscientious about appropriate and ethical conduct in the workplace assesses his or her possible self in taking credit for the entire team differently than someone with the self-schema of feeling good when presenting team work as his or her own work. This example demonstrates the overpowering impact of self-concept on someone's information processes (how they create meaning). As Markus (1990) highlights, "structures of the self are front and center in the meaning-making process" (p. 242).

According to Cameron (1999), one's current selves set the context for the possible-selves. In other words, the results or end-states people see for themselves are influenced positively or negatively by their current identities—individual or social. In a similar vein, views regarding one's abilities to attain specific goals are influenced to an extent by identities—personal or social.

Ibarra (2007), however, defines identity as possible-selves, which is particularly significant when examining contexts in which achieving a desired end-state depends on giving up the course related to one's current identity. She further advocates that people elaborate possible-selves as they adjust their activities and social associations and construe life events through the filter of shifting possibilities—well-elaborated possible-selves motivate change. We argue that these can act as potential drivers.

Also, certain possible-selves are viewed as significant for the self-concept, especially ones that are linked to the prospect of becoming or fearing to become something in the domain which is core to the self-concept (Erikson, 2007).

CHAPTER 4

# Exploring the Reservoirs of Drivers and Blockers (Conscious and Unconscious): Worldviews and Emotions

*...our souls may be consumed by shadows, but that doesn't mean we have to behave as monsters.*
Emm Cole, in the 'The Short Life of Sparrow'

## 4.1 Worldviews

A worldview is "a person or group's conscious beliefs and conceptions of the world" (O'Brien, 2013, p. 310). People view the world differently based on their own perspectives as well as the focus they put on different entities, problems and rules as individuals and in groups. Schlitz, Vieten, & Miller (2010, p. 19) believe that it "combines beliefs, assumptions, attitudes, values and ideas to form a comprehensive model of reality… encompass[ing] formulations and interpretations of past, present and future". Worldviews impact the way one perceives and analyzes events, the way one views issues and how one finds solutions to the same. In other words, these influence all facets of the way people comprehend and engage with reality (O'Brien, 2013). As such, worldviews can impact a person's adaptations to change. They shape the space in which people function, influencing their responses as per their "beliefs and assumptions".

This is also synthesized and expanded in the work of Carole Dweck (2006) on mindsets, that is, people's beliefs—conscious as well as unconscious—that they carry about themselves. People with a "fixed mindset" believe that their character, intelligence and ability are fixed, immutable attributes which cannot be altered. They see inherent intelligence as a predictor of success and challenges as "tests" of their intelligence (Blackwell, Trzesniewski, & Dweck, 2007; Heyman & Dweck, 1998; Mueller & Dweck, 1998). On the other hand, people with a "growth mindset" see failure as an opportunity to learn rather than a sign of low intelligence. They actively seek input that can translate into learning and action (Blackwell et al., 2007; Heyman & Dweck, 1998; Mueller & Dweck, 1998). These insights are particularly important for business and education.

We contend that worldviews can act as drivers as well as blockers in an individual's change efforts. When resisting change, a person's worldviews might be providing a distorted view of reality compared to what they really wish to change. Becoming embedded and subliminal with time, these fixed views can act as blockers. Healthy worldviews, on the other hand, can act as drivers, in helping individuals understand the implications of change, especially when the change is positive and leads to benefits. An example is of individuals whose worldview is an "open approach towards life", who are lively and receptive to others and different perspectives. These individuals tend to be open to change, approachable, receptive of others' points of view and acknowledge their own shortcomings. By contrast, a worldview that is "closed and defensive" might act as a blocker. These individuals are less open to criticism, react defensively and tend to be resistant to change.

The notion of worldviews as blockers shares similarities with the concept of "Ontological[1] Constraints" introduced by Erhard, Jensen, & Granger (2011). Erhard et al. (2011) differentiate these constraints into two types: Ontological Perceptual Constraints and Ontological Functional Constraints. Ontological Perceptual Constraints stem from someone's web of unevaluated views, notions, beliefs, predispositions, prejudices, socio-cultural influences and "assumptions" taken as "truths" about oneself and the world around oneself. These constraints restrict and influence the person's perceptions of their situations. As such, if someone continues with these constraints (especially during change), then they have to manage the misrepresentation of the situation at hand (Erhard et al., 2011).

---

[1] Ontology refers to our assumptions on the nature of reality and what we think reality is, whether it exists, what its components are and their interdependency.

An example of an Ontological Perceptual Constraint as a blocker we witnessed in one of our executive course participants is that of Steve,[2] a director in an oil company whose development objective was to be more inclusive with his peers. Steve came from a cultural background where seniority is highly valued, and questioning of authority is unaccepted, resulting in limited communication among managers and sub-ordinates as well as peers. Steve was not open to listening to people who wouldn't communicate in his communication style. Furthermore, he habitually *"used to think ahead and form a view faster than his peers"*, as a result of which he spent most of his energy *"defending his view rather than understanding others' point of view"*. Steve held a belief that his peers were *"missing the point"*, or "maybe" they do not understand what is required to deal with the situation at hand. Steve's "assumption" of *"my way is the optimum way"* acted as a constraint, giving him a distorted picture, influencing his perceptions and behaviors and making his peers less accepting of him.

With regard to "Ontological Functional Constraints", the behavior that results from these can be referred to as a "knee-jerk reaction" (Erhard et al., 2011). Psychologists also call this the "automatic stimulus/responsive behavior", where some stimuli may produce an unavoidable response, which is the automatic way of being and acting. Neuroscientists call many of the Ontological Functional Constraints as "amygdala hijacks"[3] (Erhard et al., 2011). When stimulated in a change resistance situation, one's Ontological Constraints and worldview can direct one's being, behavior and actions. These constraints restrict and influence the person's "opportunity set" for their being, behaviors and actions. Therefore, the optimal way of being and appropriate actions are usually not available to individuals (Erhard et al., 2011).

However, one can consciously step in and intervene in these situations (like knee-jerk reactions or amygdala hijacks), which is called a "free won't" by the neuroscientists (Jeffrey & Gladding, 2011). For example, when a thought comes to us insisting that we perform some action, we have the power to say no. This power to veto or negate is the power of free will. Jeffrey Schwartz and Sharon Begley (2002) in *The Mind and the*

---

[2] An example from our research (see Sect. 10.1, Example 3).
[3] Daniel Goleman (1996) introduced the term "amygdala hijack" in his book *Emotional Intelligence: Why It Can Matter More Than IQ*. He builds the construct of "amygdala hijacks" on the work of LeDoux (1992) on emotions and the amygdala.

*Brain* (see pp. 290–322) summarize that "free will" as "free won't". The whole idea is to have more conscious thought, an increased awareness, so as to not adhere to one's worldview or be more accommodative of other worldviews. In the business world, amygdala hijacks are not a rare occurrence and can cause serious damage to people's reputation and standing, for example, Meg Whitman's[4] shoving incident (Stone, 2010) and Steve Ballmer's[5] chair-throwing episode (Benjamin, 2014).

As an example, take Andrew,[6] a senior executive in a consumer goods company, with whom we worked. Andrew was a victim of amygdala hijacks triggered by his worldview. Andrew's development objective was to "*maintain self-control particularly in conflict situations*". Andrew had a habit of "*communicating aggressively with peers whenever there was a disagreement*". His aggressive behavior stemmed from his fear of "*losing control*" and not being listened to. Andrew also held a belief that if he did not respond the way he did, it would reflect "*compromise*", which according to him displayed "*weakness and lack of leadership*". This belief acted as a blocker—a constraint, restricting his ability to manage his aggressive emotional reaction in conflict situations.

## 4.2 Emotions

Emotions are described as "an organized and highly structured reaction to an event that is relevant to the needs, goals or survival of an organism" (Watson & Clark, 1994a, p. 89). Once stimulated, emotions entail a tendency to react in a specific manner, "action tendency". Smith & Kirby (2000, p. 90) define emotions as "a sophisticated well-being monitor and guidance system that serves both attention-regulatory and motivational functions". Emotions are not just linked to subjective experiences but expressions that signal an individual's condition to other people (Leary, Koch, & Hechenbleikner, 2001).

Some scholars (e.g. Feldman Barrett, 2004; Frijda, 2000) use the terms emotions and feelings interchangeably, although we note others (e.g. Antonacopoulou & Gabriel, 2001; Solomon, 2003) differentiate between the two. For example, Solomon (2003) argues that feelings have a physi-

---

[4] Former CEO of eBay.
[5] Former CEO of Microsoft.
[6] An example from our research (see Sect. 10.1, Example 4).

ological element and tend to be less complex than emotions which are strongly rooted in cognition. In the same vein, Parrott (2002, p. 342) believes emotions encompass a broad repertoire of psychological tendencies, such as "appraisal, readiness to think and act in certain ways, physiological changes, and social signals and dispositions, as well as feelings". In this book, we will be using emotions and feelings interchangeably.

### 4.2.1 *Emotions in Our Lives*

Gilbert & Choden (2013) claim that emotions direct people's lives by guiding their motives. The authors explain this through the example of an individual who wishes to be a world-renowned musician. This individual will put his energy into practicing more often. They will feel positive emotions when they do well in practice and may experience negativity when they don't; they will experience positive emotions when they get accepted to perform in a concert and frustration when they don't. Emotions fluctuate in keeping with the status of someone's motives and objectives. A person's motives, however, operate on a long-term basis, whereas their emotions tend to be short lived (Gilbert & Choden, 2013).

Emotions play a critical role in the working of the mind and brain in dealing with issues, especially when one is faced with the uncertainties of circumstances (Smollan, 2009), that is, during change. The sense of control that one gets from logically assessing different elements involved in certain situations (i.e. during change) is restricted. As a result of this, one might not even carry out or finish a task. An attribute of change resistance is that the information provided by emotions and the intrinsic world prevails over information that comes from the conscious or from the external world (Bachkirova, 2011).

In psychoanalytical theory, emotions and emotionality are considered to be under the umbrella of "affect" (English & English, 1958, p. 15; Rycroft, 1995, p. 4/46), and though we might be consciously aware of them as they become apparent, what stimulates the "affective impulse" is the mind, the dynamics of which are inaccessible to an individual.

According to Fineman (1993a, p. 3), psychoanalytical and psychodynamic theories are predicated on an approach developed by Sigmund Freud to study emotions as surfacing from the *unconscious* and *hidden* domain of personal anxieties, dilemmas, uncertainties and desires. This is where we are "unaware of some of our most basic motivations and feelings; they are repressed, pushed from consciousness, because of the anxiety, guilt or shame arising from the events with which they are associated" (Fineman, 1993b, p. 24). This is also similar to mental control, which looks into how people shift from seeking or avoiding thoughts to the suppression or realization of them (Wegner, 1994).

The psychodynamic approaches to studying organizational dynamics highlight a repertoire of emotions which surface when people begin dealing with constructs of identity, power, conflict and, particularly for the purpose of our research, change (Carr, 1999, 2001). Carr (2001) believes that the mechanisms involved in the individual-organization association are innate, mainly unconscious, closely linked to the construction of identity and possess an emotional aspect. He further suggests that change dislocates identity, resulting in anxiety and stress. The psychoanalytical lens with regard to change is also believed to provide valuable knowledge into individuals' emotional reactions as they are involved in "denial, avoidance and resistance" (French, 2001, p. 485). Antonacopoulou & Gabriel (2001) believe that the psychoanalytical research has concentrated more on uncertainty and unreasonableness. They maintain that individuals try to resolve contradictory emotions during times of change.

### 4.2.2 *Emotions and Change*

Emotions are also seen as an important element of the unconscious, which is merely delineated as feelings, emotions and thoughts that lie beyond one's conscious awareness (Matlin, 1995). With regard to change resistance, unconscious processes are seen as defense mechanisms that surface automatically as a reaction to *feelings* of psychological threat and are endorsed by individuals to mitigate negative *emotions* (such as anxiety) (Andrews, Singh, & Bond, 1993), which act as blockers.

Negative emotions (anxiety, in particular, which is core to psychoanalytical theory) do not just result from external threats but may also be intrinsic (intrinsic resistance) to an individual (Bovey & Hede, 2001). This intrinsic resistance usually results by priming of prior events, fears or uncertainties that an individual has faced (Bovey & Hede, 2001). This resistance comes into force as a result of tension between the residents of the subconscious[7] (i.e. thoughts, feelings, emotions, etc.) and the new residents of conscious awareness (new thoughts, feelings, emotions and intentions to espouse or act) (de Board, 1978, 1983).

These subconscious influences can impact an individual's behaviors more than conscious influences (Carole & Tavris, 1996; van der Erve, 1990). The patterns in the subconscious are not existing feelings or views in that particular moment or time but rather have been formed with time through recurrences and reinforcements and preserved in memory (Altorfer, 1992). As such, people form numerous intrinsic defense mechanisms to guard themselves from negative emotions such as anxiety (de Board, 1978).

As an example from our research, think about Aaron,[8] a business head, whose development objective is to increase his self and social awareness, in other words, emotional intelligence. Aaron confesses that he doesn't "*acknowledge his feelings before acting*" and doesn't "*pay attention to stakeholders' emotions*". The emotions that are driving Aaron's behavior and acting as a blocker in his objective of increasing his emotional intelligence include "*fear of becoming less business oriented*" if he pays attention to people's emotions and "*fear of being perceived as manipulative and a politician*".

Another example is Emma,[9] a seasoned executive in the banking sector. Emma's development objective was to manage her time well and manage her boundaries. She described it this way: "*I want to manage my boundaries. I am open to everyone and everything. As a result, I can't manage my time*". Emma used to "*give in to all requests*" and would find it difficult to take tough but right business decisions if they affected people negatively. The emotions that were blocking her efforts to make the change included her intrinsic feelings of becoming "*unapproachable*" and being perceived as "*proud and arrogant*" if she changed.

---

[7] Like Freud, we use the terms "conscious" and "unconscious" interchangeably in our work. An interesting article on the use of these terms by Michael Miller (2010) of Harvard Health Publishing can be found at: https://www.health.harvard.edu/blog/unconscious-or-subconscious-20100801255

We also recognize that there is debate about the terms in scholarship. For example, Malim & Birch (1998, p. 205) define subconscious as "one level below conscious awareness" and believed that unconscious is "a total lack of awareness" (Malim & Birch, 1998, p. 204).

[8] An example from our research (see Sect. 10.1, Example 5).

[9] An example from our research (see Sect. 10.1, Example 6).

Although emotions can have an adverse impact, making emotions the "scapegoat" for all negative perceptions of a person and separating these from the process of decision-making is not helpful. Agreeing with Guy (2005), "Emotions may sometimes be misleading; but to respond by trying to bleach out thought of their emotional colors is not bright at all".

The success of the conscious is quite often sabotaged by powerful emotions that can lead to chaos in all major accomplishments (Bachkirova, 2011; Bovey & Hede, 2001). As such, the conscious separates, downplays, controls and takes different steps to guard itself from powerful emotions (as discussed earlier). Emotions might be viewed as resulting from external events and therefore, "the way to be happy is by fixing the world in place so that it does not go awry and upset me" (Claxton, 1994, p. 194).

Emotions, especially positive emotions, can also act as drivers, by managing, stimulating and helping people achieve what is needed. Emotions can enable an individual to solve significant issues when interacting with their surroundings (Leary et al., 2001). Emotions are reflected in events significant to individuals' welfare, making them concentrate on concerns that necessitate their urgent attention. Certain emotions motivate individuals to embrace adaptive behaviors (Leary et al., 2001), for example, satisfaction, contentment, optimism and so on.

As positive emotions hint at benefits for the individual, while negative emotions act to the contrary, an individual might be inclined toward behavior that is beneficial (Leary et al., 2001). However, we note that the vast majority of research in this area shows otherwise—that people focus on negative emotions (e.g. Bovey & Hede, 2001; Carr, 2001; Frijda, 2000; Huy, 2002). The dichotomy resulting from this research demonstrates the value of exploring both drivers and blockers.

In Emma's case (discussed earlier), the positive emotions of feeling proud for managing her time well and feeling confident from taking the right decisions (which she surfaced during her exploration exercise) could act as drivers, helping her to accomplish her developmental objective and making the necessary change she wants.

Emotions also form a critical basis of one's intelligence (Goleman, 2004; Mayer & Salovey, 1997). In the current business world, many organizations are increasingly acknowledging the value and role of emotions and encouraging the development of emotional intelligence in employees (e.g. Palmer, Walls, Burgess, & Stough, 2000; Prati, Douglas, Ferris,

Ammeter, & Buckley, 2003; Scott-Ladd & Chan, 2004). The notion of emotional intelligence demonstrates a shift from simple resentment against emotions to acknowledging their significance. Yet this concept is predicated on the reasoning of the conscious (i.e. intelligence) and not the entire individual. It is centered on the benefits of emotions (Bachkirova, 2011).

Emotions offer distinct views and ways of looking at the world compared to what the conscious has access to. They form a communication channel between the conscious and unconscious (Bachkirova, 2011). Therefore, engaging with emotions is significant for engaging with the unconscious, which can help in overcoming resistance blocker behaviors and accomplishing change with positive drivers. There can also be a relationship between emotions and their somatic expression in the body. This has been seen, for example, in coaching and development work on leadership presence and communication undertaken by one of the authors with senior executives. A range of nonverbal and verbal exercises first expose significant performance gaps (such as an overly closed body, voice articulation problems or ineffective eye contact). Then a series of specific advice is given, and the person tries out direct changes in the movement (to be video viewed later). Beyond the communication coaching, as part of the leadership development debriefing, the person voices their positive emotional response to watching these changes, as well as the emotional concerns they would have if they made these changes to their ongoing presence. In this way, both drivers and blockers can be confirmed and confronted in their development plan.

Emotions form a communication channel between the conscious and unconscious. The success of the conscious is quite often sabotaged by powerful emotions that can lead to chaos and an inability to change. In other words, even if we make a conscious decision to change, we can still get swayed by emotions which can overpower us and can disrupt the entire change process. This is where emotions act as blockers. Emotions, however, act as drivers as well, by managing, stimulating and helping people achieve what is needed and desired. Emotions, however, also form a critical basis of one's intelligence and can enable an individual to solve significant issues when interacting with their surroundings.

As an example, we conclude this chapter with the case of Thomas,[10] an executive, whose developmental objective was to grow his business unit by

---

[10] An example from our research (see Sect. 10.1, Example 33).

utilizing and encouraging "out of the box" thinking. He had previously resisted seeking out group engagement and involvement with innovation decisions, particularly excluding newer or more junior members. Now Thomas routinely conducts meetings with junior associates and managers in his unit to discuss ideas and do brain storming. Because of his friendly and understanding behavior, he tends to give constructive feedback to his juniors, who at times propose nothing new or "out of the box", but rather general suggestions. Since he started this initiative, about a quarter of the company's new products have come from their unit, which he sees as a "success" and validation of the initiative. For him, his emotional intelligence including empathizing and seeking out ideas or feedback acts as a driver, helping him accomplish his innovative objective while sustaining employee engagement.

We have seen a significant number of executives where their worldviews (how people perceive and hold beliefs) and/or their emotions are either significant drivers or blockers, and sometimes both. These are both substantial reservoirs and sources to be explored for leadership development change efforts.

CHAPTER 5

# Exploring the Reservoirs of Drivers and Blockers (Conscious and Unconscious): Big Five Personality Traits

> *You cannot defeat darkness by running from it, nor can you conquer your inner demons by hiding them from the world. In order to defeat the darkness, you must bring it into the light.*
> Seth Adam Smith, in Rip Van Winkle and the Pumpkin Lantern

Personality can be defined as "an individual's characteristic patterns of thought, emotion and behavior, together with the psychological mechanisms—hidden or not—behind those patterns" (Funder, 1997, pp. 1–2). These patterns communicate one's choices, likings and wishes and impact behaviors which are stable across contexts and which differentiate one individual from another (Vakola, Tsaousis, & Nikalaou, 2004).

Self-awareness, as discussed earlier, refers to one's ability to be aware of the features of self (Hall, 2004), and personality traits constitute an important component of the self. We believe that understanding and recognizing variations in personality can provide crucial insights for leadership development, enabling people to identify and mitigate the gaps between what is required of them and their capacity to deliver; find solutions that will nurture them; and manage or avoid stressful situations. These directly relate to potential drivers and blockers.

Therefore, in this chapter, we review literature on the Big Five personality traits: (agreeableness, extraversion, conscientiousness, neuroticism and openness). Our field research shows that these are most likely to act as

© The Author(s) 2019
I. C. Woodward et al., *Exploring Leadership Drivers and Blockers*,
https://doi.org/10.1007/978-981-13-6276-7_5

drivers or blockers in an individual's change efforts. Each of these is explained in turn, and the hypothesized associations between these and a person's change efforts, drivers and blockers, are discussed.

## 5.1 Personality Traits: The Five Factor Model

The role of the personality Five Factor (agreeableness, extraversion, conscientiousness, neuroticism and openness) Model (FFM)[1] in predicting people's motivation and behavior is well demonstrated by research (Hogan & Holland, 2003; Judge & Ilies, 2002). Classic and current studies in a variety of disciplines acknowledge the FFM as a comprehensive model which sums up and explains the crucial and consistent individual variations in personality (Barrick & Mount, 1991; Costa & McCrae, 1992; Fleeson & Gallagher, 2009; Judge, Simon, Hurst, & Kelley, 2014). With regard to change, research (e.g. McCrae & Costa, 1986; Vakola et al., 2004) has employed the FFM model to examine individual attitude toward change.

A detailed overview of the Big Five personality traits, including descriptions as well as relevant previous research, is provided in Table 5.1. We also provide direct examples from our own research of how these personality traits act as drivers or blockers in a person's change efforts. Based on our review of the research, we believe that these five personality traits can encourage individuals to direct, accept and oppose change. In other words, they can act as drivers as well as blockers in determining people's change efforts. However, they might work together with other factors such as emotions, values, worldviews and the like, and potential interrelationship is an area we identify in our conclusion for further research related to drivers and blockers.

Beyond the "Big Five", there are a number of other personality traits, dispositional variables and characteristics that are associated with change, assumptions and forces that can also act as drivers and blockers, which we explore in the next chapter.

---

[1] We use the NEO-PI version of the FFM for this book. In addition, in Sect. 10.5, we provide a comparison for reference, with the Myers-Briggs personality indicators because that instrument is so widely used in managerial training and development.

**Table 5.1** Big Five personality traits—drivers and blockers examples from our research

## Agreeableness

**Description**

The propensity of an individual to interact in a manner ranging from being compassionate to antagonistic. It delineates the degree to which one is understanding and friendly versus unfriendly, independent, detached and cold (McCrae & John, 1992; Vakola et al., 2004).

**Previous related research**

Agreeableness is associated with a positive attitude toward change (Vakola et al., 2004). Studies suggest that individuals with higher agreeableness levels are more hesitant to oppose change and are more inclined to adopt new procedures and policies (Lee-Baggley, Preece, & DeLongis, 2005; McCrae & Costa, 1986). Research, however, suggests that agreeableness is not a predictor of job performance (Barrick & Mount, 1991) and is also not significantly correlated to leadership (Judge, Bono, Ilies, & Gerhardt, 2002).

**Examples of higher and lower agreeableness as drivers**

(b) Alex (Example 8) is an associate in a professional services organization, whose objective is to maintain commitment to the team that he has been recently assigned to, replacing one of the previous members. Since Alex is new in the team, he's considered an *"outsider"* and has been intentionally excluded from a few informal team meetings by some of his team members. However, because of his agreeable and flexible nature, he has been able to put aside the negatives and focus on achieving the team objectives. This personality trait is serving as a driver in maintaining his engagement with the team.

(d) Ali (Example 10), a physician, has a very high reputation as a doctor but at the same time is seen as cold and unfriendly. Ali believes that it is important to be "to the point" with his patients who otherwise start giving him a "whole bunch of irrelevant stories", which affects his efficiency. He believes that if he is friendly with his patients and shows his compassion, it would interfere with the way he operates as a doctor. In his case, low agreeableness acts as driver helping him work in an efficient and clinically focused way.

**Examples of higher and lower agreeableness as blockers**

(a) Higher agreeableness, however, can act as a blocker too. Emma (Example 7) is an executive in the banking sector, whose objective is to manage her time and boundaries and not give in to all requests. Emma has a helpful and compassionate personality (i.e. her agreeableness) that makes her feel bad when taking the right decision if she sees that decision affecting someone negatively. The personality trait of higher agreeableness is acting as a blocker in her change efforts.

(c) Kenneth (Example 9), a banking executive, is very rational but lacks agreeableness and is often perceived as unsympathetic. Once called a "jerk at work", he tends to be overly critical and dismisses any proposed ideas, feedback, information and change. With this approach, he cuts off the communication lines between himself and others. His disagreeable nature acts as a blocker leading to a lot of issues and negatively affecting the workplace dynamics.

*(continued)*

**Table 5.1** (continued)

### Extraversion

#### Description

The extent and magnitude of social engagement and activity. It specifies the degree to which one is sociable, assertive and outgoing versus quiet, shy, reflective and solitary (McCrae & John, 1992; Vakola et al., 2004). The extraversion/introversion distinction is also seen in relation to the source of mental energy, where introverts are seen drawing energy from within, whereas extraverts obtain it from others and the external environment (Leonard & Straus, 1997).

#### Examples of extraversion/introversion as blockers

(e) Martin (Example 11) is a general manager in a consumer goods organization, whose development objective is to be a better networker and who is trying his best to make this change. Martin accepts that *"being more socially engaged will help him gain better access to quality information, which will help him create more value for himself, his business and others"*. He, however, finds it *"unnatural to reach out to people for no apparent reason"* and does not make the time for social engagement. Martin scores *low on extraversion*, he is an introvert. This trait is acting as a blocker in his attempt to make this change.

#### Previous related research

Extraversion is associated with a favorable attitude toward change (Vakola et al., 2004). There is a consensus in the literature that the demonstration and communication of positive emotions lie at the heart of extraversion (Watson & Clark, 1997). Individuals with positive emotions are more supportive of change than the ones with negative emotions (Vos, 2006). Research suggests extraversion as a positive predictor of job performance (Barrick & Mount, 1991; Bing & Lounsbury, 2000; Johnson, 1997) and leadership emergence and effectiveness (Judge et al., 2002). However, studies also show that introverts are better leaders than extraverts in unpredictable environments and in leading proactive teams (Grant, Gino, & Hofmann, 2010).

#### Example of extraversion/introversion as drivers

(f) Thomas (Example 12) is an executive in an energy organization, whose development objective is to develop his business unit by encouraging "out of the box" thinking. Thomas regularly arranges meetings with junior associates and managers in his unit to discuss ideas and do brain storming. However, in these meetings, he does more listening than talking, a norm which he follows even in his personal life. He is able to leverage the talents of the people around him and trains them to improve on their thinking and reach their full potential. Thomas scores low on extraversion and sees it as the reason for his increased engagement with his employees. This trait of his allows ideas from his business unit to blossom into new products. About a quarter of the company's new products come from their unit. His introversion acts as a driver helping him accomplish his objective.

(*continued*)

Table 5.1 (continued)

| | |
|---|---|
| (g) John (Example 13), a business head in the banking sector, sees introversion and extraversion as "powerful" mechanisms that impact people's approach toward work. He admits being an extravert and acknowledges that he often comes across as "*powerful and dominating*". His extravert nature makes it difficult for him to deal with his extravert peers, who also seek to dominate discussions. He humorously describes their interaction as "*every now and then there is an explosion*". In case of John and his peers, extraversion is acting as a blocker in their efforts to work together and actively listen. | (h) Fred (Example 14), an operations executive in the financial services sector, had been given a responsibility to head his organization's restructuring initiative in a subsidiary located in a different country. Fred was advised on the importance of building networks and personal relationships with the key contacts in the host country before he started in his new role. This way of working was different to the one Fred was used to, which didn't require him to build networks to get work done. However, his outgoing extravert personality which facilitates an active social interaction acted as a driver for him to build his network and achieve his objective. |
| **Conscientiousness** | |
| **Description** | **Previous related research** |
| Conscientiousness: The level of perseverance, organization and drive in one's behavior oriented toward accomplishing tasks. It describes the degree to which one is efficient, reliable, organized and diligent versus disorganized, careless and indolent (McCrae & John, 1992; Vakola et al., 2004). | Conscientiousness is associated with favorable attitude toward change (Vakola et al., 2004). Research has shown conscientiousness to be a significant factor in how people evaluate and react to stressful situations (e.g. Lee-Baggley et al., 2005). High conscientiousness has also been related to performance (most stable predictor) (Barrick & Mount, 1991; Salgado, 1997), commitment to challenging goals (Barrick, Mount, & Strauss, 1993) and the use of effective coping mechanisms (Connor-Smith & Flachsbart, 2007). However, some studies suggest a negative correlation between conscientiousness and managerial promotability (linked to factors like flexibility, innovation, persuasiveness), which is different to performance (Robertson, 2000). |

(*continued*)

**Table 5.1** (continued)

| Examples of higher and lower conscientiousness as blockers | Examples of higher and lower conscientiousness as drivers |
|---|---|
| (i) Laurel (Example 15) is a manager in a software organization, whose objective is to facilitate her team's development and finish projects on time. As it happens, Laurel is a quite disciplined, hardworking individual who has high standards. She is often seen as a *"perfectionist"*. Because of this trait, her team members are hesitant and delay approaching her when they experience problems which further leads to work delays. This trait acts as a blocker, making it difficult for her to achieve her objective. | (j) Returning to the Example 14 case of Fred (Example 16) here. Being given the opportunity to head his organization's restructuring initiative, Fred was very aware that *"it will not be an easy task"* and that he will not be welcomed by the subsidiary organization. However, Fred took it as a challenge to prove himself to the top management team. The high conscientiousness levels in Fred which makes him disciplined and achievement-oriented acted as driver helping him achieve his objective. |
| (k) Richard (Example 17) is a case writer, whose objective is to meet his deadlines for submission of cases and other related research work. Richard however concedes that he is quite disorganized and is *"a procrastinator"*. As such, he focuses less on working and finishing tasks *"leaving things to tomorrow"*. Being low on conscientiousness acts as a blocker, delaying his submissions and affecting his performance. | (l) Christina (Example 18), a system analyst, scores low on conscientiousness. Although she is frequently disorganized, she is highly regarded by her peers for creativity and spontaneity. Her manager wants her to take more responsibility for a new project development, so that she can use her sense of creativity and spontaneity to arrange a series of IT experiments with her team. Being aware of her deficiencies, she has been given an administrative support to work closely with her. For her, the trait of low conscientiousness manifested through her creativity and spontaneity acts as a driver to enjoy the process while achieving results. |

(*continued*)

**Table 5.1** (continued)

## Neuroticism

### Description

The propensity of an individual to experience negative emotions, for example, anxiety, uncertainty, fear, anger and depression. It is also referred to as emotional stability and defines the extent to which an individual is fearful, anxious and stressed versus calm, stable and self-assured (McCrae & John, 1992; Vakola et al., 2004).

### Examples of higher and lower neuroticism as blockers

(m) Mary (Example 19) is an administrative staff member in an educational institution. Mary's objective is to develop herself and be more collaborative with her colleagues. Mary, however, is a pessimist and tends to over-react in most situations. As such, her coworkers see her as an *"over-sensitive"* individual-someone who is difficult to work with and therefore avoid dealing with her. This trait contributes as a blocker in her efforts to improve her collaboration with her colleagues and to develop herself.

(o) Peter (Example 20), an investment banker, is a self-assured individual who is excessively certain at times to the extent of being over-confident. Being self-assured and very calm acts as a blocker for him as he does not invest time in monitoring and planning and therefore frequently fails to evaluate the riskiness of his valuations and investment decisions.

### Previous related research

Research suggests that neuroticism is associated with negative attitude toward action and an inclination toward inaction (Ireland, Hepler, Li, & Albarracin, 2014). Negative attitude toward action however is mediated by anxiety in individuals who score high on neuroticism (Ireland et al., 2014). Furthermore, studies found a negative correlation between neuroticism and job satisfaction (Judge & Locke, 1993; Tokar & Subich, 1997), job performance (Judge, Higgins, Thoresen, & Barrick, 1999) and leadership effectiveness (Judge et al., 2002). However, research also suggests that highly neurotic individuals can perform better than their stable colleagues when expending large amounts of effort (Smillie, Yeo, Furnham, & Jackson, 2006).

### Examples of higher and lower neuroticism as drivers

(n) In Mary's case, although she is viewed as *"oversensitive"* and *"temperamental"* by her colleagues, she is a hardworking and an organized individual. Her feelings of insecurity and anxiety—the fear of performing badly—are able to also serve as a driver for her, making her work hard on her projects and thereby develop herself.

(p) Victor (Example 21), a senior project lead, is a very calm and emotionally stable individual who has developed and maintained an aura of approachability with the people around him. His nature helps him maintain positive working relationships at work, thereby driving success. Being low on neuroticism acted as driver for him during the recent economic crisis, when his team looked up to him for assurance and hope.

*(continued)*

**Table 5.1** (continued)

## Openness to experience

### Description
The tendency to actively look for novel experiences. It defines the degree to which one is curious, flexible, artistic and creative versus being cautious and enjoying following routines (McCrae & John, 1992; Vakola et al., 2004).

### Previous related research
People who are less open tend to have strong opinions and remain committed to those opinions (Flynn, 2005). With regard to change, research has linked openness to change to adapting to and dealing with change. In particular, research (e.g. McCrae & Costa, 1986) shows a positive relationship between openness to experience and using effective coping mechanisms. As such, openness to change, as an aspect, is related to favorable attitude toward change (Vakola et al., 2004). Research also links openness to task performance and creativity (Raudsepp, 1990; Rothmann & Coetzer, 2003). To the contrary, research by Hayes, Roehm, & Castellano, (1994) found that successful employees scored less on openness to experience in relation to less successful employees.

### Examples of higher and lower openness to experience as blockers
(q) Laurel (Example 22), because of her strong discipline, is less flexible and less open to experience, which negatively impacts the entrepreneurial spirit and creativity of her team members. Being less open to experience acts as a blocker in her efforts to develop her team.

### Examples of higher and lower openness to experience as drivers
(r) Kathy (Example 23), a senior operations executive in the logistics and supply chain management sector, is very routine-oriented and structured. She was given responsibility to manage a major restructuring initiative that involved implementation of a new logistics infrastructure in her organization. With her strict adherence to structure, she made sure that all the deadlines were met, tasks were clear and every team submitted a weekly progress report to the management. This trait acted as a driver in helping her ensure smooth functioning as the new initiative was implemented.

(*continued*)

**Table 5.1** (continued)

| | |
|---|---|
| (s) Greg (Example 24) is a senior sales executive in a machinery and equipment industry, working for an engineering company dealing with a variety of clients. Greg has a risk-taking attitude, which stems from his openness to experience trait. His working approach is less detail-oriented, making him pay less attention to the standard working procedures. Openness to experience acts as blocker for him in dealing with his company's clients with strong protocol adherence such as hospitals and army. | (t) Mark (Example 25) is a writer, whose objective is to continue publishing new and interesting pieces. Mark is fascinated by different cultures and life styles. He habitually travels a lot to increase his knowledge and experiences which help him produce works that are new and inspiring. Being highly open to experience serves as a driver, which helps him achieve his objective. |

See Sect. 10.1 for the source of the examples

CHAPTER 6

# Exploring the Reservoirs of Drivers and Blockers (Conscious and Unconscious): Other Personality Traits and Characteristics

> *You get to love your pretence. It's true, we're locked in an image, an act—and the sad thing is, people get so used to their image, they grow attached to their masks. They love their chains.*
> Jim Morrison, lead vocalist of 'The Doors'

## 6.1 Self-Esteem

Self-esteem represents a universal dispositional feature related to an overall perception of self-efficacy and worth (Judge, Thoresen, Pucik, & Welbourne, 1999). Research suggests that high levels of self-esteem are linked with low levels of stress or better coping with stress during change (Ashford, 1988; Callan, Terry, & Schweitzer, 1994). Self-esteem is seen as a key need of the individual (Maslow, 1954), although not just for its own purposes.

Self-esteem reflects the need for belongingness, to be acknowledged by others and be regarded as one of them (Bachkirova, 2011). Research by Leary, Tambor, Terdal, & Downs (1999) indicates that self-esteem is related to anxiety about interpersonal rejection and social marginalization. Leary et al. (1999) sought to understand why people struggle with self-esteem: whether the struggle provides protection against anxiety or ambiguity; whether it boosts their goal accomplishments or whether, perhaps, the struggle is just for the sake of it. However, their conclusion is predicated on a fundamental belief about human nature:

Because solitary human beings in a primitive state are unlikely to survive and reproduce, psychological systems evolved that motivated people to develop and maintain some minimum level of inclusion in social relationships and groups. (p. 89)

Concerns about self-esteem are common for the first level of ego in adult development (Bachkirova, 2011), that is the "socialized mind", where it can act as a blocker, although Kegan (1982) would contend that the term "self-esteem" is not relevant for people even at this stage, since their "esteem" rather than stemming from the sense of "self" comes from what others think. At the second stage (i.e. "self-authoring mind"), self-esteem issues are unlikely to be as pronounced. They might, however, at times surface as confidence issues that one may face, with regard to accomplishing a specific task or performance, and also signal a need for improved judgment about objectives, aspirations and the world (Bachkirova, 2011).

A good example is Adriano,[1] a divisional CEO in a news and information agency. Adriano's developmental objective is to improve his relationship with others. Adriano, however, exhibits negative dominant behavior and concedes that he's "*not open to criticism*" and has "*unrealistic expectations of others*". He holds the belief that being more open to everything—feedback, dialogue, people and so on—will "*limit his freedom*" and he will no longer be in "*control*". These factors are central to his own view of his self-esteem and are acting as a blocker in his efforts to make the change in his behavior and achieve his objective of improving his dynamics with others.

Self-esteem, however, when under check, can act as a driver for this self-authoring stage. In research, high self-esteem is associated with a number of positive behaviors such as persistence at challenging jobs (Shrauger & Rosenberg, 1970), satisfaction (Diener, 1984) and less neuroticism (Robins, Hendin, & Trzesniewski, 2001). In the case of Fred[2] (a case we discussed in the previous chapter), his positive self-view and the self-confidence that he could head the restructuring initiative acted as a driver in helping him accomplish his objective.

Self-esteem issues are more prominent for people at the "unformed ego" (socialized mind) stage. "Unformed ego" (socialized mind) requires help from other people as well as from the norms and standards set by

---

[1] An example from our research (see Sect. 10.1, Example 31).
[2] An example from our research (see Sect. 10.1, Example 26).

them. Individuals at this stage are not prepared to deal with new circumstances without depending on already familiar and acknowledged rules or recommendations from other people. This results in a gap between how an individual sees him or herself and the expectation of him or her (Bachkirova, 2011). We believe that self-esteem, here, may be seen as a blocker, a discrepancy between what is required from an individual and what he or she can actually do. Issues of low self-esteem may surface if people are worried about not being accepted by others because they may be unable to fulfill others' expectations.

Let us take, Roger,[3] a senior executive in an energy infrastructure organization. Roger's developmental objective is to be more assertive with his team. Roger, however, feels very hesitant to voice his opinions openly when he is uncertain. He believes that he "*will lose credibility, if he's not always right*" and "*will be perceived as unfriendly*". He also sees himself as "*compromising too much*" and feels "*blocked*" when faced with "*unfamiliar situations*". Roger's excessive focus on other people's perspectives and their approval shows that he has a "socialized mind" (see Kegan & Lahey, 2009), associated with self-esteem struggles. His low self-esteem here is acting as a blocker, preventing him from speaking up, and impeding his objective to be more assertive with his team.

There are two other views on the nature of self-esteem offered in the literature: the self-consistency motive and the self-enhancement motive (Baumeister, 1993, 1999; Mruk, 2006). The self-consistency motive steers people to look for information that reinstates their beliefs (positive or negative) about themselves. It may be difficult to deny or alter these views about oneself once they are established. The self-enhancement motive on the other hand steers people to gain information that portrays them positively and ignore information that might reflect negatively on them. As such, self-esteem is marked with the potential for distortion (Claxton, 1994; Dunning, 2006), and numerous studies show various ways people may protect themselves against attacks to their own self-assessment[4] (Fingarette, 2000; Goleman, 1997).

In some people, self-esteem (as the overall value that one places on oneself as a person) signals their current state with regard to how they

---

[3] An example from our research (see Sect. 10.1, Example 27).
[4] This is similar to the construct of confirmatory bias in decision sciences (see Evans, 1989; Plous, 1993), which refers to people's propensity to deliberately disregard or neglect information inconsistent with their beliefs.

perceive they are being accepted and acknowledged by others, in case they need support to overcome their resistance behaviors. We see high self-esteem (when in check, i.e. not over-confidence or hubris) as a motivational force, a driver influencing someone's behaviors and helping them to bring about the change desired. For example, Emma,[5] who we highlighted earlier when discussing emotions, also tapped into a strong personal drive for increasing her self-worth as part of her achieving her development objective. Low self-esteem, on the other hand, can essentially be seen as a blocker, making one believe change is a threat and evoking resistance behaviors and attitudes.

## 6.2 Locus of Control

Locus of control as a dispositional variable is employed to demonstrate the variations in the manner information is understood and analyzed (Hyatt & Prawitt, 2001; Tsui & Gul, 1996). Locus of control refers to one's beliefs of one's capacity to apply control over the context (Rotter, 1966). Individuals with an internal locus of control see themselves having control over their destiny, while the ones with the external locus of control see the role of powerful forces such as luck, chance or fate in exercising control over their lives (Cobb-Clark & Schurer, 2013; Furnham & Cheng, 2016; Lefcourt, 2013; Rotter, 1966).

Research indicates that individuals with an internal locus of control actively look for information relevant to the task, in comparison to the individuals with the external locus of control (Organ & Greene, 1974; Pines & Julian, 1972; Seeman, 1963). For example, Seeman (1963) suggested that the active information-collecting tendency of the individuals with an internal locus of control was apparent only when the information under consideration was pertinent to significant goals.

This, Seeman (1963) believed, could be because individuals with an internal locus of control may recognize the importance of information for accomplishing the goal faster than their external counterparts. Further, he argues that individuals with an internal locus of control are clearer in their objectives and values than ones with an external locus of control, and therefore tend to actively respond to the opportunities that support those goals (Chong & Eggleton, 2003).

---

[5] An example from our research (see Sect. 10.1, Example 6).

With regard to change and the uncertainty associated with it (Ashford, 1988; Callan et al., 1994; Nelson, Cooper, & Jackson, 1995), an individual's sense of control over the context will affect his or her psychological response to change (Chen & Wang, 2007). The association between locus of control and organizational change is indicated by studies, with most of them linking an internal locus of control with better adjustment (Ashford, 1988; Israel, House, Schurman, Heaney, & Mero, 1989) and effective coping mechanisms (Anderson, 1977; Callan et al., 1994). In other words, studies suggest that having a more internal locus of control enables people to better manage unfavorable environmental influences (Callan et al., 1994).

We contend that the belief that one has control over one's destiny (internal locus of control) can act as a strong driver—a motivator enabling an individual to apply more effort in making the change or achieving his or her objective. Individuals with an external locus of control, on the other hand, are less likely to be motivated to make an effort to produce the change. For them, the drive to initiate change takes a back seat to influences that are seen to be beyond one's control. Here, the external locus of control acts as a blocker, impeding one's change efforts.

We explain this through the example of Barbara,[6] a manager in a consumer goods company. In a group coaching session, she explains the reasons why she received low ratings in several leadership dimensions of her 360° feedback. Her observation and perception of her situation is that she's a victim of the environment as well as other people affecting her ability to exercise her leadership effectively. She feels that everything is outside her control and refuses to take any ownership of her leadership approach. In exploring her drivers and blockers, her coach and group mates help make her aware of her strong external locus of control. Developing self-awareness about her default victim position was the first step in her moving toward a more internal locus of control and thereby drive change.

## 6.3 SELF-EFFICACY

Self-efficacy[7] is a "belief in one's capabilities to organize and execute the courses of action required to produce given attainment" (Bandura, 1997, p. 3). Unlike locus of control which refers to an individual's beliefs about

---

[6] An example from our research (see Sect. 10.1, Example 28).
[7] Self-efficacy is different from self-esteem which "represents a self-perception about one's competence and value"

their capacity to implement the necessary reaction, which ensures achieving the desired results, self-efficacy pertains to whether the outcomes of these endeavors are within one's control (Bandura, 1997).

There are a number of ways through which self-efficacy might influence one's change efforts. The concept of self-efficacy draws in a "mobilization or motivational component" that enables the adjustment of behavior to match the changing situations (Gist & Mitchell, 1992). Furthermore, research (e.g. Schunk, 1983) has observed that self-efficacy is specifically prominent in situations that are considered new and stressful to people. Lower levels of self-efficacy, on the other hand, are associated with "defensive behavior", for example, resistance or protecting turf (Ashforth & Lee, 1990).

These studies indicate that high levels of self-efficacy can act as a driver in change efforts, while low levels are a blocker. In other words, people with high self-efficacy are more likely to be optimistic about their commitments to tasks or change challenges; for example, the idea that "When I commit to a task or take up a challenge, I am positive that it will be successful" or "I can accomplish it if I put my heart and head into it". Whereas people with lower levels of self-efficacy are more likely to feel less confident of their own ability to make the change, that is the idea that "I feel that I am not up for it".

Self-efficacy (as one's estimate of one's fundamental ability to cope, perform and be successful), which taps into positive determination, can act as a powerful driver for supporting change. One example is Sylvia,[8] a divisional head in a hospital, who we worked with a few years back, and who demonstrated self-efficacy characteristics of high confidence and high result focus. Sylvia at that time was in charge of an event that was supposed to take place in her organization in a couple of weeks' time. Sylvia, however, had to manage it jointly with a colleague she was "*not fond of*" and who had a "*completely different working style*". Both individuals, however, had similar strong personas and displays of confidence. Although they had a different skill set, they were both results driven as a display of their confidence. As such, Sylvia determined to be able to put aside their other differences and work constructively with her colleague toward making the event a success. Here Sylvia's positive self-efficacy acted as a driver helping her to accomplish her objective.

(Donald & Pierce, 1998, p. 51).
[8] An example from our research (see Sect. 10.1, Example 32).

We note that in the commentary of this chapter we treat self-esteem, self-efficacy and locus of control as distinct areas and that there is debate in the literature on their relationships to one another.[9]

## 6.4 Positive and Negative Affectivity

Positive affectivity is a key personality disposition, mainly demonstrated in features such as optimism, confidence, enthusiasm, well-being and affiliation. It is broadly linked with the positive worldview (Judge et al., 1999). A research study by Bowman & Stern (1995) found positive affectivity to be positively correlated with coping strategies (such as problem solving and problem reappraisal) in stressful work situations.

Likewise, research by Holahan & Moos (1987) suggests personality traits of confidence and easy-going disposition are significant predictors of effective coping with regard to life events. As these traits denote significant aspects of positive affectivity, it can be expected that high levels of positive affectivity will act as a driver in an individual's attempt to change. That is, people with high positive affectivity levels will be inclined to look for ways to proactively change for betterment (Duffy, Ganster, & Shaw, 1998) (i.e. "If I improve, it will be much easier for me to manage and this will help everyone—me as well as others").

Negative affectivity, on the other hand, has been defined as a personality characteristic manifested in attributes such as negative emotional states (Kaplan, Bradley, Luchman, & Haynes, 2009; Watson & Clark, 1984). Negative affectivity is linked with distress and involves an individual's tendency to concentrate on negative aspects (Bowman & Stern, 1995; Penney & Spector, 2005). Bowman & Stern (1995) also found a positive correlation between negative affectivity and avoidance coping indicating that their use might lead to an increase in negative emotions in the workplace. As such, we believe negative affectivity can act as a blocker in an individual's change efforts. In other words, negative affectivity meddles with the thinking needed for achieving goals and objectives (Frisch, 2006) (i.e. "I feel that no good outcome will come out of the process" or "I don't think making a change is possible or worthwhile" or "Even if I put in effort, I might not be able to cope with the change process").

---

[9] Although the majority of the studies (e.g. Abouserie, 1994; Horner, 1996) treat these constructs in isolation, research by Judge, Erez, Bono, & Thoresen (2002) suggests that measures that assess self-esteem, locus of control, neuroticism and generalized self-efficacy are strongly related and may be the indicators of the one latent higher order construct.

## 6.5 Risk Aversion

Risk aversion refers to the tendency of people to look for (risk seeking) or keep away from risky situations (Kahneman & Tversky, 1979). A research paper by Maehr & Videbeck (1968) on risk aversion found that risk-averse individuals are less likely to take chances and are more likely to get distressed in situations where risk was prominent. This was further confirmed by studies conducted by Cable & Judge (1994) and Judge et al. (1999). Since change is often perceived as taking risk, individuals who are risk-averse might view new and risk-related situations negatively. For them, risk aversion acts as a blocker in achieving a change or making a decision.

An example of this is Shirley,[10] a senior lecturer, working in a university that had switched to a different web application (an e-learning platform) from the one it used earlier to support contemporary pedagogy. This initiative was not welcomed by Shirley, and like most of her academic friends, she was uncomfortable using it. She believed she "*had invested a lot of effort in mastering the old system, and it was working well*". The change would mean that she would "*have to spend a lot of time understanding and learning about it, and changing her materials*". She also believed that she would "*feel stressed*" if she could "*not look professional to her students when operating it*" or "*if something goes wrong*" (there is a risk of accidentally sending incorrect information to students for which she would be held accountable—not the IT area). This risk-averse attitude stemmed from an apprehension of change, fear of feeling stress and concern about risking her reputation. This served as a blocker, impeding commitment and effort to adopt, embrace and accept the change.

The willingness to take risks (risk seeking), on the other hand, may increase the probability that individuals explore options and initiate change perceived as upsetting the status quo, which might act as a driver, especially when change is important. For example, when confronted with an uncertain decision-making scenario, risk-seeking individuals will normally take a courageous stand, so as to increase the prospects of getting the best out of the potential opportunities. In the example of Thomas[11] we quoted earlier, in addition to his emotional intelligence, he surfaced risk-seeking characteristics as positive drivers to innovate, thus supporting his initiative to engage more people in the creativity process—rather than constrain those involved.

---

[10] An example from our research (see Sect. 10.1, Example 29).
[11] An example from our research (see Sect. 10.1, Example 33).

Research (e.g. Stewart & Roth, 2001) suggests that entrepreneurs exhibit higher risk-seeking behaviors than company managers. Organizations operating in contexts in which entrepreneurial spirit is critical and where it thrives through ideas, products and so on will be more willing to take risks. Individuals in these organizations would be more oriented to change the status quo, be more creative and take risks to attain results that are exceptional. For them, the risk-seeking trait will act as a driver, helping them deal with the challenges posed by the dynamic or ever-changing environment.

Based on the above discussion, we contend that people's tendency in terms of their willingness to take risks or avoid taking risks can act as a driver or a blocker in determining their response to change, that is, how they lead it or deal with it.

## 6.6 Tolerance for Ambiguity

Tolerance for ambiguity can be regarded as a propensity to see ambiguous circumstances as desirable. On the contrary, intolerance of ambiguity implies that the encounter with ambiguity is threatening (Budner, 1962). High tolerance for ambiguity in leaders has been linked to planning and market orientation; in other words, it facilitates the planning process in challenging and ambiguous situations (Westerberg, Singh, & Häckner, 1997).

An early study by Rydell (1966) showed that tolerance for ambiguity is related to people's willingness to modify their views on issues and how they will endure and deal with novel situations. According to Barringer (2008), individuals with a high tolerance for ambiguity can deal with novel and ambiguous situations with less difficulty in comparison to ones with low tolerance for ambiguity. With the uncertainty, anxiety and stress associated with change, we believe that a low tolerance for ambiguity can act as a blocker in an individual's attempt to change.

Take the case of Laurel,[12] whose objective is to facilitate her team's development and finish projects on time. Laurel, besides being less open to experience, has low tolerance for ambiguity that causes delays in her team's project completion times. Because of her low tolerance for ambiguity, she is less willing to make plans or decisions predicated on partial information or contradictory data. She is not convinced that

---

[12] An example from our research (see Sect. 10.1, Example 30).

these decisions or plans (based on partial information) will lead to good results and therefore struggles when it comes to enhancing team work and building trust. Low tolerance for ambiguity acts as a blocker in Laurel's case, making it difficult for her to achieve her objective/s in the context. We note that for someone else, in a very different situation, if the behaviors were reflecting high levels of conscientiousness, this could be a driver if the situation was extremely high risk, where the consequences of wrong decisions would be catastrophic.

We believe high tolerance for ambiguity, on the other hand, can operate as a driver, especially in the current, dynamic and disruptive business world, which at times requires leaders to make quick decisions based on incomplete information, as is suggested by Westerberg et al. (1997). Leaders with a high tolerance for ambiguity and confidence that their actions or decisions will lead to successful results are more likely to get better at making accurate predictions on how things function or will function, and will also be good at enhancing and building trust in teams. In the same vein, research by Teoh & Foo (1997) indicates that entrepreneurs with higher tolerance for ambiguity can better deal with stress in their role, resulting in better performance results. All in all, tolerance for ambiguity can act as a major factor; a driver in assisting and dealing with the stress and challenges associated with change, complexity and volatility; or as a blocker, making people uncomfortable with change, and thereby impeding their efforts, and those of others.

## 6.7 OTHER POTENTIAL AREAS RELATED TO DRIVERS AND BLOCKERS

Throughout this chapter, we examined a wide range of personality traits and dispositional variables and their potential roles as drivers and blockers to add to the dispositional perspective in leadership development. These characteristics included self-esteem, locus of control, self-efficacy, positive and negative affectivity, risk aversion and tolerance for ambiguity. Although we note that some traits tend to be more stable over time, such as the Big Five (Costa & McCrae, 1985), some are more adaptable (Judge et al., 1999), such as positive/negative affectivity.

However, there are other areas related to personality traits and behavioral patterns that we see surfaced as examples and descriptors of drivers and blockers in executives we work with. An example is the trait of "drive" in business leadership, put forth by Kirkpatrick & Locke (1991), which, according to them, comprises aspects such as *achievement motivation, ambition, energy, tenacity and initiative,* all of which are indicative of elevated effort level (p. 49)—as well as goal (Heilbrun Jr & Friedberg, 1988; Hudson, 2014) and result orientation (Rosenman et al., 1964). It could also include behavioral patterns such as Alpha (Type A) and Beta (Type B) (see e.g. Friedman & Rosenman, 1974; Ludeman & Erlandson, 2006, 2007; Mahajan & Rastogi, 2011; Matthews & Saal, 1978; Ward, Popson, & DiPaolo, 2010).

For the purposes of exploring change drivers and blockers in senior leaders in this book, we have not included these different forms of behavioral patterns as reservoirs, as they may be behavioral reflections more than sources. Nevertheless, some of the authors are undertaking further research on these matters, subject to later publishing. This type of research is also called for in our conclusion.

Also raised in the conclusion is another ongoing area of field research about the question of life experiences in relation to drivers and blockers. This work is intended to look at life experiences and their influence on the sources of drivers and blockers in relation to a specific development objective. For example, we have seen a large number of positive and negative early life experiences (such as parental interactions) emerge as important reasons during the exploration process in relation to sources of drivers and blockers such as self-esteem, motivation and values. This will be clearly seen in the mini cases of Chap. 8 and Sect. 10.8.

Nevertheless, besides the personality traits and dispositional variables covered in the past two chapters, our personal values and motivators (both extrinsic and intrinsic) constitute other important psychological characteristics that can serve as drivers or blockers in an individual's change efforts. We explain these in the next chapter.

# CHAPTER 7

# Exploring the Reservoirs of Drivers and Blockers (Conscious and Unconscious): Values and Motivators

*It's strange, but wherever I take my eyes, they always see things, from my own point of view.*
*Ashleigh Brilliant (Pot Shots No 266)*

## 7.1 Values

Values are the "fundamental principles or standards—the essential elements of an individual, which guide his or her thinking, emotions, behaviors, actions and choices over time, and across multiple situations" (Woodward & Shaffakat, 2014, p. 21). They are also defined as a motivational influence (Martha, 1976), which can promote or impede an individual's efforts in accomplishing a task.

Values "are hierarchically organized in terms of their importance for self" (Feather, 1995, p. 1135). Bardi, Lee, Hofmann-Towfigh, & Soutar (2009) note that people vary in the importance they place on values as well as their personal value hierarchies. A value significant to one individual may not be as significant to another. Rokeach (1973) and Shalom (1992) both highlight the critical role of personal value hierarchies in shaping perceptions, attitudes and behaviors.

Conflict of values (intrapersonal, interpersonal or organizational) is one of the causes of resistance behaviors (Hultman, 2006; Jenny, 1996; Williams, 2011)—thus becoming blockers. Embedded values and principles can prevail over the outside reality, "creating string effect and conviction of truth without any configuration from the environment—feeling over fact—and then having the neo-cortex (conscious) rationalize the choice" (Wade, 1996, p. 123).

Values exist in people's conscious and unconscious, and create both desires and fears (Woodward & Shaffakat, 2016). Values have been linked to decision-making, including decisions on what objectives one should undertake (Parks & Guay, 2009). Furthermore, they enable individuals to behave with regard to how they see themselves, the circumstances they face and their course of action at a particular moment in time (Woodward & Shaffakat, 2014). Values may differ, especially in terms of their significance and clarity (Feather, 1995). Because they are so fundamental, an individual fights any attempts to alter them and reacts positively or negatively when these values are either satisfied or breached (Woodward & Shaffakat, 2016).

A person's values act as lenses of perceptions, helping them to see different entities in their surrounding in different ways (Bachkirova, 2011). They comprise beliefs that people hold, which in turn guide their behaviors and actions. These beliefs, which are rooted in societal norms and basic individual wants and desires, go beyond certain events and states and have an obligatory touch to them (Feather, 1995). What we propose is that values can influence someone's choice of developmental objectives as well as their achievement. That is, some human values can act as drivers and some as blockers in efforts to achieve change objectives. Let us explain this through the examples of Martin[1] and Emma[2] (both cases discussed earlier).

Martin's developmental objective is to be a better networker. He, however, finds it *"unnatural to reach out to people for no apparent reason"* and does not make time for social engagement. Martin holds the "assumption" that *"networking is political, manipulative and evil"*. His "assumption" stems from his values of *"Integrity"* and *"Transparency"*. Martin puts it this way *"I believe networking involves taking and giving favors which affects one's integrity"*.

His values of maintaining integrity and transparency are acting as a blocker for him in his efforts to become a better networker, although he accepts that *"being more socially engaged, will help him gain better access to quality information, which will help him create more value for himself, his*

---

[1] An example from our research (see Sect. 10.1, Example 35).
[2] An example from our research (see Sect. 10.1, Example 36).

*business and others*". However, other values that he holds, which he describes as "Recognition" and "Achievement", could act as drivers, helping him understand, and then believe, that by being good at networking, he will receive "*recognition which would lead to achievement*".

Emma's objective, on the other hand, was to manage her time and boundaries. Yet, she was struggling to make this change, as she used to "*give in to all requests*" and would feel uncomfortable taking the right decisions if she saw those decisions affecting someone negatively. Emma's core values which explained her "assumption" of "*I believe they need me*", which she described as "*self-fulfillment by touching lives*", "*caring about relationships*" and "*being generous*", acted as blockers, making her "*give in to all requests*" and not to say "*No*". However, other values she holds, which she defines as "*Inner peace*", "*Honesty*" and "*Respect (by telling people what you think)*", could also act as drivers, helping her understand and then believe, that by "*being more assertive and firm when taking the right decisions*", she will attract more "*respect*" and it would also help her "*create more time*" for herself.

We also note that at times, the same value for a person can be both a driver and a blocker depending upon their change objective. Imagine a person whose core values include "loyalty". This person has two development objectives. The first is to increase their active listening. The second is to be able to make difficult or tough people-related decisions. For the first objective, "loyalty" can act as a driver to motivate better and loyal relationships achieved through active listening. However, for the second objective, perceptions of loyalty might screen out more objective assessments of performance and act as a blocker.

In our experience, where people have undertaken values articulation and exploration exercises in executive education programs and coaching, the articulation and awareness of their values is very powerful in assisting their understanding of their reactions to different situations, in particular change—and values very frequently emerge in using the "Drivers and Blockers Exploration Tool" as well (see Chap. 8 and Sect. 10.8 mini case examples).

## 7.2 Extrinsic and Intrinsic Motivators

Another set of characteristics that can act as drivers and blockers is the range of both extrinsic and intrinsic motivators that can cajole or force people into achieving their change objectives or engage in resistance behaviors. Similar to other deep-seated reservoirs, an intensive exploration of these constitutes an important step in helping individuals move from envisaging change to deciding on and acting on it.

The term motivation is inherent in the definition and various theories of leadership and other related concepts. Motivation is a force that energizes, directs and sustains goal-oriented behaviors (Cleveland & Murphy, 1992). Over time, various motivational theories have emerged, focusing on different aspects of human behavior. We focus on motivational theory by Herzberg (1959) and self-determination theory by Ryan & Deci (2000), which are most relevant to the research of this book. Herzberg's (1959) theory differentiates motivation factors into extrinsic and intrinsic motivation, with intrinsic stemming from an individual and linked to efficiency and self-actualization and extrinsic originating from external factors and associated with social reward (Lawler, 1973; Pinder, 2014).

Likewise, self-determination theory differentiates between *extrinsic* motivation and *intrinsic* motivation, where the former pertains to carrying out an action as it leads to separable consequence; and the latter pertains to carrying out an action because it is intrinsically stimulating and satisfying (Deci & Ryan, 2010). For example, an employee might be motivated to take a training program to learn new skills as he or she knows the value of acquiring new skills or because learning a new skill is important for performing new responsibilities in his or her new role (Ryan & Deci, 2000). In other words, motivation results because an individual highly regards an activity or due to external forces. Individuals can be forced to act by a personal interest or even a bribe—their behaviors can be guided by their personal commitment to stand out or by the fear of being monitored. These instances of being motivated internally or by external forces are well-known (Gagné & Deci, 2005; Ryan & Deci, 2000). Deci (1976) has also emphasized the significance of the joint role of extrinsic and intrinsic factors in performance, which is confirmed by a recent meta-analytical study conducted by Cerasoli, Nicklin, & Ford (2014).

Similar to the construct of extrinsic and intrinsic motivation, Friedlander & Walton (1964) proposed a related construct of positive and negative motivation, where positive relates to elements core to the work process, such as work interest, significance of work, challenging work and autonomy (sources of satisfaction); and negative relates to elements which are external to the work process such as remuneration and compensation, living expenses, superior's views, leadership and management and housing (sources of dissatisfaction). These characteristics, according to Friedlander & Walton (1964), are similar to the ones found in research by Herzberg, Mausner, & Snyderman, (2009) showing that some work elements are crucial for and result in satisfaction (though not dissatisfaction), that is, intrinsic motivation, while other work elements are crucial for and result in dissatisfaction (though not satisfaction), that is, extrinsic motivation.

Based on these motivational theories and work from Taylor (2012), who suggests that individuals are motivated toward their change objectives by different motivators, we suggest a motivation matrix (see Fig. 7.1) related to drivers and blockers and their positive and negative attributes, respectively.

- **Extrinsic-positive**: *Acknowledgment and recognition, position, economic rewards, professional advancement (potential result: some change, partial fulfillment, dependent on others for continued change and positive feelings).*
- **Intrinsic-positive**: *Setting and achieving goals, autonomy, control, mastery, aspiration, passion/purpose, fulfillment, self-confidence, self-actualization (potential result: successful change, personally motivated fulfillment).*

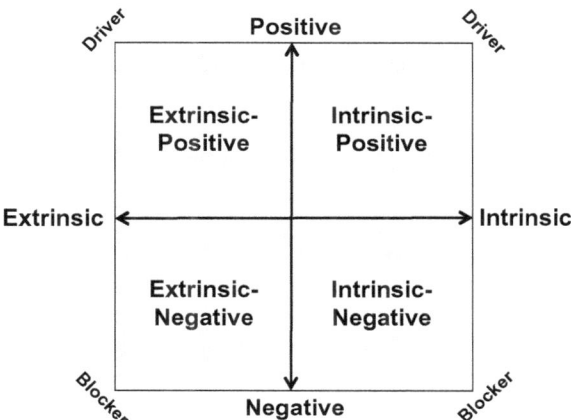

**Fig. 7.1** Motivation matrix. (Derived and adapted from Herzberg (1959), Ryan & Deci (2000) and Taylor (2012))

- ***Extrinsic-negative***: *job insecurity, insecurity in relationships, financial and social pressure, career uncertainty (potential result: some short-term change, high risk of relapse).*
- ***Intrinsic-negative***: *Threat, anxiety, uncertainty, personal insecurity, fear of failure, low self-efficacy (potential result: some change with trepidation, possible relapse, difficult to sustain with its personal emotional toll).*

We also note that the "intrinsic-positive" motivating drivers we suggest have congruence with those suggested by the popular business author, Daniel H. Pink in his 2009 book, *Drive: The Surprising Truth About What Motivates Us.* He suggested three motivational elements in business practice: (1) autonomy—the desire to direct our own lives; (2) mastery—the urge to make progress and get better at something that matters; and (3) purpose—the yearning to do what we do in the service of something larger than ourselves.

The four motivation clusters shown in the matrix (Fig. 7.1), we believe, can act as drivers as well as blockers in people's commitment to change. An individual's reasons that lead them to engage in resistance behaviors might differ with regard to the motivation types that give rise to them. The intrinsic-positive motivation, where the motivation stems from a sense of strength and security, is the ideal motivation type (Taylor, 2012), a driver, and so is the extrinsic-positive motivation, whereas the others, that is, intrinsic-negative or extrinsic-negative, are the potential blockers, which can impede someone's efforts in making the change.

For example, consider Andrew,[3] a director in a consumer goods company (a case discussed earlier) whose development objective was to "*maintain self-control particularly in conflict situations*". Andrew's fear of not being in control—the intrinsic-negative motivation—and the fear of being perceived as weak if he compromises— the extrinsic-negative motivation—acted as blockers in his efforts to achieve his objectives. However, at the same time, he held the motivation of being recognized as a good leader, which he puts as "*Good leadership drives diverse teams to better decisions*"—the extrinsic-positive motivation—and had the drive toward achievement—the intrinsic-positive motivation—both of which could act as drivers, helping him achieve his objective.

---

[3] An example from our research (see Sect. 10.1, Example 37).

It should also be noted that where people hold more than one of these motivations simultaneously, they could be driven by the one that is more powerful in comparison to the others. The same might be determined by other factors such as values, attitudes, emotions and social constraints. A potential area of future research is to examine the possible interrelationships and interplay of the different reservoirs and sources of drivers and blockers. It might also be that they are not necessarily related and are just different factors responsible for action/inaction and may vary among people. This topic is another area for future research in drivers and blockers that we raise in the conclusion.

## 7.3 Summary of the Reservoirs and Sources of Drivers and Blockers

Our review across Chaps. 3, 4, 5, 6, and 7 of different potential sources of drivers and blockers shows a wide range of elements that might influence a person's change behaviors. These drivers and blockers (see Sect. 10.6 for a summary table of the sources and issues) were drawn from an extensive academic literature review and examples from our research and field work (see the list in Sect. 10.1).

In this review, we looked into the dynamics of conscious and unconscious, which act as reservoirs of drivers and blockers, such as mini-selves, possible-selves, worldviews, emotions, personality traits and dispositional variables, values and extrinsic and intrinsic motivators (see Fig. 7.2 below). Following Freud, we contend that behavior stems from the continuous interaction of sometimes-conflicting influences that are often operating outside one's awareness.

In summary, we reason that what drives a person toward action or inaction with regard to achieving one's objectives resides to a significant extent in one or more of these factors. We have also begun to explore the potential link between these factors to better understand different perspectives that can help us understand and analyze people's change behaviors. With an understanding of the reservoirs and sources of drivers and blockers, the background of adult development and the relationship of self-awareness to leadership development, we turn to applying these ideas in practice.

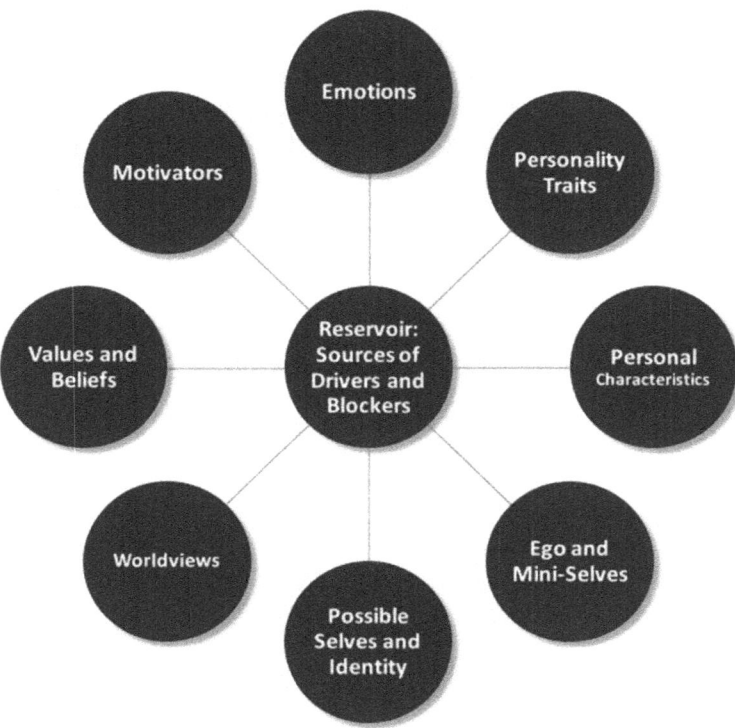

**Fig. 7.2** Reservoir: conscious and unconscious sources of drivers and blockers

## CHAPTER 8

# Uncovering, Understanding, Unleashing, Overcoming: Exploring Drivers and Blockers in Leadership Development Practice

> *People need to know that they have all the tools within themselves. Self-awareness, which means awareness of their body, awareness of their mental space, awareness of their relationships—not only with each other, but with life and the ecosystem.*
> Deepak Chopra

## 8.1 The "Drivers and Blockers Exploration Tool"

As a contribution to leadership development practice, we created the "Drivers and Blockers Exploration Tool" (2018 Version), with four detailed examples as mini case studies from our field research (see Sects. 10.7 and 10.8), to uncover an individual's drivers and blockers—connected to a defined leadership aspiration, specific development objective(s) and context. Using the tool within our programs and coaching work has provided a robust platform to observe and test potential benefits of exploring both drivers and blockers, especially where these are set against specific personal leadership development objectives, and within an integrated and complementary set of other development activities and interventions.

Similar research in a global executive program, where deeper exploration of hidden assumptions was conducted, found that participants were generally able to identify some kind of change blockers (Dominé, 2012). About two-thirds of the development objectives were so-called relational-based objectives, which "target an improvement in how the participants interact with others in the most general sense, whether this involves getting along better with co-workers, being more forceful with them or understanding them better" (Dominé, 2012, p. 47).

Although exploring drivers and blockers is primarily an individual exercise, we note that it can also be carried out in group situations that provide a psychologically safe environment for the kind of intensive awareness exploration in which executives can engage in courageous conversations with each other; and help each other challenge some of their assumptions. In addition, there is the potential for groups or teams to collectively explore their drivers and blockers. Future research might report on such explorations and the adaptations required to our methodology to effectively undertake such an exploration across a group or team level.

In our earlier leadership development workshops with senior executives, we had used adapted versions of Kegan & Lahey's (2009) "four-column exercise". In these, leaders and executives examined their "competing commitments" and "immunity to change", allowing blockers to emerge as they examined the big assumptions underlying why they were not accomplishing their change objectives. This approach focused on aiding participants to become much more aware of the negative emotional influences (which are really "change blockers"), such as fears, that stop them from achieving their leadership development objectives. Surfacing these is very important, because it opens up the possibility for participants to develop ways of overcoming them. Our experience with the four-column exercise created a fundamental and foundational basis for the tool we developed for exploring both drivers and blockers, and we acknowledge that our work acts as an extension of Kegan and Lahey's groundbreaking processes and research.

The tool, now trialed with more than 2000 executive participants, explores change drivers that might motivate them, in addition to exploring blockers, through 4 progressive phases and 14 progressive steps (see Fig. 8.1 below). The psychodynamic reflection and surfacing methods in the tool and method also allow for integration with other leadership development work, such as coaching, feedback and sustaining a personal development agenda.

So, at a deeply personal level, using an integrated exploration, the tool helps surface profound insights—that connect both drivers and blockers. After identifying blockers in relation to their specific leadership development objective(s), the tool can then help leaders uncover and surface different perspectives (positive projections for the future as well as underlying

> ### Drivers and Blockers Exploration Tool – Overview (2018 Version)
>
> The tool and surfacing method are structured in 4 Phases and 14 Steps, as follows:
>
> #### Phase 1:
> #### Leadership Aspiration and Specific Development Objective
>
> Steps 1 and 2 outline the leadership aspiration or vision, and then define the specific development objective and its rationale for change.
>
> #### Phase 2: Exploring Your Blockers
>
> Steps 3 to 6 progressively examine behaviors, negative emotions, fears, reasons, assumptions, personal characteristics (including values, beliefs, attitudes, personality and other traits) and life experiences that can create blockers, and then surface these in relation to the development change objective set.
>
> #### Phase 3: Exploring Your Drivers
>
> Steps 7 to 10 progressively examine behaviors, positive emotions, positive benefits, reasons, assumptions, personal characteristics (including values, beliefs, attitudes, personality and other traits) and life experiences that can create drivers, and then surface these in relation to the development change objective set.
>
> #### Phase 4: Insights, Commitments and Actions
>
> Steps 11 and 12 encourage deep reflection, drawing together insights and understandings as a result of uncovering the drivers and blockers and then allow a restatement of the leadership aspiration and development objective, together with proposed commitments and actions to "unleash the drivers" and "overcome the blockers". Steps 13 and 14 allow further reflection to consider the insights in the wider setting of the person's broader leadership. Here consideration is given to whether drivers might become blockers in other circumstances; and to whether any of the blockers might shift to being drivers as strengths in different circumstances or situations.

**Fig. 8.1** Drivers and blockers exploration tool overview (2018). (Published with kind permission of the authors © I.C. Woodward, S. Shaffakat and V.H. Dominé (2018). All Rights Reserved. Section 10.7 provides the full tool, its steps and its questions)

negative assumptions), spinning their perception of their situation in a positive light (i.e. what could happen if they overcome the blockers). From this, they recognize the drivers that can motivate them to overcome their blockers. In other words, it helps individuals uncover their biggest drivers while confronting their blockers—and imagining how these might become drivers.

Importantly, the fourth phase of the exploration process restates the person's leadership aspiration and development objective, together with their commitments and actions, based on the insights generated relating to both drivers and blockers. Leaders can also consider how to leverage the drivers to their advantage, and turn blockers into potential strengths across other leadership situations and contexts.

During the exploration exercise, people converse with themselves, documenting and articulating the issues faced in achieving their developmental objectives. This personal reflection is a tangible reality, helping the individual pinpoint the role of drivers and blockers in different aspects of their life, work, leadership/management approach, relationships, as well as the interplay between them. We see broader personalization benefits arising for executives articulating their drivers and blockers, and then seeing the implications for other aspects of their leadership beyond the specific development objective. The writing down of answers also concretely helps bring unconscious matters to light.

Exploring "drivers and blockers" is ideally done with the assistance of development professionals or as part of a well-designed development program, course or coaching process. Our tool helps undertake this process, but it can also be modified or adapted as needed by leadership development professionals. The profound insights generated in this surfacing process should significantly influence the personal leadership agenda action plan and commitments made. By systematically exploring drivers and blockers, a leader can unleash the power, force and impetus of drivers to support and propel their desired change; and to overcome the blockers that screen out, obstruct or stand in the way of their desired change. Generating the profound insights from this reflection and articulation gives an extraordinarily deep understanding for working on the very personal aspects of an individual's leadership—as can be seen in the four mini cases of Sect. 10.8).

We do not use the phrase "competing commitments" in our tool because we found that many executives in cross-cultural settings strongly resisted using the term, as they regarded the notion of "commitment" as an integral part of their leadership development agenda—a positive affirmation. However, we acutely know the value of the term as it applies to the work of Keegan and Lahey and the "competing" elements they highlight. We are certain that their groundbreaking work will continue to be used extensively in coaching and leadership development work into the future.

Nevertheless, the words drivers and blockers resonated extremely easily with contemporary global business executives in our fieldwork—and were relatively straightforward to comprehend and use—especially as we are combining both concepts in the tool.

Consistent with our literature review, we argue that exploring drivers and blockers can help people progressively move to higher "orders of mind", and growth. We acknowledge the vast array of effective leadership development approaches available today. We suggest that the explicit incorporation of exploring drivers and blockers (and the potential use of the tool and surfacing method) should be highly complementary to a wide range of important leadership development methods in current usage in executive development. Indeed, this exploration is inherent or implicit in many cases (such as immersive self-awareness with coaching and feedback).

To demonstrate how widely the concept we advocate might be applied, we include Sect. 10.9, which connects exploring drivers and blockers with a selection of major leadership and development theories and approaches, including adaptive leadership (Heifetz, Linsky, & Grashow, 2009), authentic leadership (Avolio, Luthans, & Walumba, 2004), emotional intelligence (Goleman, 1996), charismatic leadership (Gardner & Avolio, 1998), immunity to change (Kegan & Lahey, 2001a), personalization (Petriglieri et al., 2011) and positive leadership (Diener, 2000; Peterson, 2000; Seligman, 1998a, 1998b; Snyder, 2000). Our purpose is not to advocate a particular approach, but show the potential importance, relevance and broad usability of exploring drivers and blockers in a wide range of future leadership development activities.

After exploring "drivers and blockers", coaching, feedback and support from others are extremely valuable. In other words, creating a support system that includes people who provide an individual with an active encouragement and advice, together with managing the "triggers" to desired or "non-desired" behaviors is indispensable.

In our field research, using the tool over time, a number of important insights emerged, that may assist leadership development practitioners with its use:

- Sufficient "time" space, with appropriate "head" and "physical" space, is highly desirable to maximize the reflection and insight generation benefits from undertaking the exploration of the drivers and blockers activity itself. (In our experience, it takes a number of hours to work through the explanations, questions and documentation of answers in each Phase in the exploration—with deliberate breaks after Phases 2 and 3. Phase 1 is sometimes done as pre-work).
- Creating an environment of psychological safety is absolutely essential to promote deep introspection, and because the exploration process can surface difficult and sometimes repressed memories.
- Being clear, precise and specific on the development objective to pursue is essential to garner maximum insights on the relevant drivers and blockers (e.g. increased active listening in employee discussions rather than a generic improvement in emotional intelligence).
- Answering the various stage questions with complete phrases, statements or sentences (rather than one-word answers) tends to enrich the understanding, clarity and nuances of the issues as these emerge.
- Participants should be discouraged from racing ahead to answer all the questions and should be given adequate reflection and documentation time step by step.
- The order and flow of the question stages has been trialed in multiple permutations, and the current version appears to uncover the most profound levels of insights based on our research to date.
- There is considerable value in undertaking the exploration exercise for the first time, after some degree of intensive reflection and feedback has occurred, and the leader or executive has been thinking about possible change seriously—and within a well-designed and integrated leadership development process.
- Many participants re-ran their exploration questions some days or some weeks later, gaining additional insights.

- Documenting the answers in a meaningful and thorough way substantially assisted the ability to update, amend and commit to leadership action plans.
- In answering the specific questions for each phase, there is sometimes overlap or duplication in some of the answers (especially between Steps 5 and 6, and Steps 9 and 10). This overlap becomes an important source of critical insights for the leader; and participants should not be concerned about having duplication.
- Undertaking Phases 1–3, where the main driver and blocker exploration work can be done, is generally well accomplished in one intensive session. However, we have seen that Phase 4 on "Insights, Commitments and Actions" likely needs much more time. We have seen great value in having the leader or executive take some time to think about this, and set another defined writing reflection and discussion period later on. This is very often successful after sharing initial observations and insights with others and getting some preliminary feedback before documenting their answers in Phase 4.
- Sharing driver and blocker insights with trusted members of the leader's support system (mentors, coaches and the like) is invaluable—and the resultant conversations usually give rise to additional insights and feelings of support in making the desired changes. Seeking explicit feedback on progress and setting up practice experiments to try new behaviors are equally crucial.

## 8.2 Drivers and Blockers Exploration in Action: The Case of Jennifer

Jennifer is the Chief Financial Officer of a specialist financial services firm. The thematic issue explored using the drivers and blockers tool and process in a major leadership development program was a lack of active listening combined with impatience in her interactions with others. Below in Table 8.1 is a mini case study which replicates her exploration, answers and insights working through all 14 questions and 4 phases of using the "Drivers and Blockers Exploration Tool" and its process. We present this as illustrative to readers of the kinds of insights and contribution to leadership development that we see emerging in these kinds of exercises. In Sect. 10.8, three more mini case studies are presented for reference and information.

**Table 8.1** Leadership development application example of the drivers and blockers exploration process
Mini case example—Jennifer[a]—female—chief financial officer, Specialist Financial Services Firm
Development objective explored: lack of active listening with impatience in interactions with others

| | Tool question | Jennifer's responses in going through the drivers and blockers surfacing methodology |
|---|---|---|
| **First phase** | **Leadership aspiration and specific development objective** | |
| Step 1 | Briefly state your overall **leadership aspiration** (or vision) for yourself as a leader into the future to be the "best leader you could be" | As a leader in the future, I am seeking to be a motivating leader of people, highly recognized for my experience, results and knowledge. I am also seeking to be seen as a business executive capable of leading the entire organization, not just my finance management area. A leader who can balance fairness with actions. |
| Step 2 | State **one** specific **development objective** for change in yourself. Also state your **rationale** for making this change in your leadership behaviors. Then, briefly explain how succeeding in this objective will help you achieve your leadership aspiration. Be explicit and focused in stating this development objective or goal rather than being too general. (e.g. "deep active listening" rather than "more emotionally intelligent" or "becoming a better leader") | Specific development objective: I need to become a deep and active listener who can successfully involve and interact with people—across different backgrounds and perspectives. The 360-degree feedback I read highlighted a lack of focused, and active listening with my team as a major problem—with lots of comments on this. There were many comments about demonstrating impatience and not taking the team with me on initiatives. There were also comments about cutting people off and seeming to be distracted. I also saw in my leadership approaches and communication preference styles diagnostics that I am heavily oriented towards directive and monitoring leadership with an extremely high level of rational/direct communication style.<br><br>My team and my peers come from very different cultural backgrounds covering many countries. I am the only person of a particular (*culture disguised*) in this group, and my culture is much more direct than all the others. |

(*continued*)

**Table 8.1** (continued)

| | Tool question | Jennifer's responses in going through the drivers and blockers surfacing methodology |
|---|---|---|
| **Second phase** | **Exploring your blockers** | |
| Step 3 | List down the **current specific behaviors** that you are doing that are preventing you from achieving your personal leadership development objective stated in Step 2. This list might include behaviors or actions that you are not doing, that are contributing to your problem or issue | I always go straight to the point and to the business matter in any discussion with someone at work and rarely talk about personal matters or ask how people are. (Absolute Opposite: I would always begin with person to person chit-chat, ask questions and show interest in the person). |
| | | I rarely ask questions in any discussion with my team members unless it is to find out about their progress on some matter. (Absolute Opposite: I would always ask questions as the opening of discussions including follow up questions). |
| | | Any questions I tend to use are like this: "Don't you think the following is the case?" (Absolute Opposite: I would ask open questions rather than using pre-decided statements in a question format). |
| | | I demonstrate my impatience by getting slightly louder and more direct or sharper in my voice and tapping my foot or hand continuously. (Absolute Opposite: I would never raise my voice and remain calm all the time in my body). |
| | | I also tend to cut people off mid-sentence or talk over them. (Absolute Opposite: I would never cut people off, allow them to finish, and not interrupt others). |
| | | I am constantly looking at my mobile phone while I talk with people, and very frequently respond to text messages whilst talking or listening. (Absolute Opposite: I would never use my device when talking and listening to other people). |
| | Next, for each current specific item in your list, put the **completely opposite behavior** for this in brackets next to each item | |

(continued)

**Table 8.1** (continued)

| | Tool question | Jennifer's responses in going through the drivers and blockers surfacing methodology |
|---|---|---|
| Step 4 | Look at the list of **completely opposite behaviors** you described in Step 3. Imagine that you are now behaving in this completely opposite way<br><br>Do you have any **concerns, fears, worries, anxieties** or any other **negative emotions, feelings or thoughts**, if you imagine yourself behaving in these completely opposite ways? If so, what are these concerns and fears? | I am very worried that changing things will waste a lot of time or miss opportunities or not pick up problems quickly. Our business is in a very competitive space and markets move extremely quickly.<br>If problems happen and I miss them, I will be blamed or described as slow.<br>I am extremely concerned that I might be negatively viewed as "too girly" or "too emotional", if I don't act with the "testosterone" we have in our business culture.<br>If I don't succeed in this job, I can never hope to get the top job, and I have a lot of future financial wealth riding on success.<br>I fear that to be less direct just isn't me and may not be worth the effort it would take.<br>I would be very uncomfortable not having my device and instant information. |
| Step 5 | What **reasons** do you have, or what **assumptions** are you making for yourself, that could explain your negative concerns, feelings or fears identified in Step 4? | You have to be fast and work hard to be ahead of the pack.<br>I work very long hours already, I can't really see how to get the time for all this people stuff and question asking.<br>Finance sector is usually very male, and there are more risks for me in getting to the top.<br>My family and I can be very well off in the future if I succeed now.<br>I just don't like being blamed for things or not being seen as a real success. I am pretty insecure.<br>I'm used to working with people who just get it and get on with it. I also prefer people who get straight to the point. |

(*continued*)

**Table 8.1** (continued)

| | Tool question | Jennifer's responses in going through the drivers and blockers surfacing methodology |
|---|---|---|
| Step 6 | Carefully consider your answers to Step 5. Think about your **personal characteristics** (such as personality, values, beliefs, attitudes, motivations) as well as your **professional and personal life experiences**. Which of these characteristics and/or experiences would explain or underpin your **reasons and assumptions** answered in Step 5? (Do not be concerned that there may be duplication of answers here compared to those above). | Rational and results focus communicator preference style.<br>Directing and monitoring leadership approach.<br>Values of Hard Work, Achievement, Recognition and Self-Direction.<br>Lots of professional experience across banking and investment—knows how to act in these environments.<br>Very strong extrovert.<br>In the program coaching, I learnt about being very "alpha" and possibly an "insecure overachiever".<br>*Note: There were some confidential personal/private life issues that emerged in this person's reflection here including their growing up with a lot of money problems and being ridiculed at school. There were also some damaging private relationship issues. Details for these are not included in the list above for privacy reasons.* |
| **Third phase** | **Exploring your drivers** | |
| Step 7 | Imagine you absolutely achieved your development objective stated in Step 2. Describe the **new or changed behaviors** you would be exhibiting. (These would be similar to those opposite behaviors you described to yourself in Step 3—but are now a much **more realistic list of behaviors**, rather than completely opposite behaviors) | Add some personal chit-chat when meeting team members and increase level of question asking.<br>Begin discussions with questions as the opening including follow up questions. Spend some moments preparing these before important discussions.<br>Would be asking a lot more open questions rather than using statements in the question format.<br>Would be controlling my voice when I start to feel frustrated and try to keep my body calmer with both feet on the floor. Also use some deep breaths—or practice "time-outs".<br>Would not be cutting people off and allowing them to finish. Should be monitoring my interruption levels. Attempting to make sure I have enough personal energy before going into important conversations where listening is needed—and this may drain me.<br>At meetings or in discussions, make a conscious choice as to whether to keep the phone on or switch it off and put it away at the beginning. |

*(continued)*

**Table 8.1** (continued)

| | Tool question | Jennifer's responses in going through the drivers and blockers surfacing methodology |
|---|---|---|
| Step 8 | Reflect upon the new or changed behaviors you described in Step 7. What are the **positive emotions, feelings or thoughts** you are likely to have, or the **benefits** you might derive or see, if you achieve this change or behave in these new ways | I think that I would be seen as responding to the feedback I've gotten and show I'm making some positive changes.<br>I think that I might be able to connect to a wider network of different people that could help my career.<br>I think that more people might like me as well as respect me.<br>I think the turnover in my team might reduce and the work stress in our team could go down.<br>I think I could sleep better if I was calmer and have some better personal relationship time.<br>*Note: Other personal private matters arose in these answers that are not reported above.* |
| Step 9 | What **reasons** do you have, or what **assumptions** are you making that could explain your positive feelings or the potential benefits identified in Step 8? | I would very much like to be seen as responsive and delivering.<br>If there are additional skills that can help the career goals, this would be positive.<br>The viewpoints and options by others about me are important to me.<br>I would show that I'm capable of doing things well in more than one way.<br>It would be a relief not to have to stay in a stressful mode all the time.<br>I would really like a personal life that was not so confrontational.<br>Perhaps I could be a different kind of female role example in my sector—yet successful.<br>Also, it is possible that a more sustaining approach to leading could be good for ensuring financial security longer term.<br>*Note: Other personal private matters arose in these answers that are not reported above.* |

(*continued*)

**Table 8.1** (continued)

| | Tool question | Jennifer's responses in going through the drivers and blockers surfacing methodology |
|---|---|---|
| Step 10 | Carefully consider your answers to Step 9. Think about your **personal characteristics (such as personality, values, beliefs, attitudes, motivations) as well as your professional and personal life experiences**. Also think about your own **strengths and talents**. Which of these characteristics and/or experiences and/or strengths would explain or underpin your **reasons and assumptions** answered in Step 9? (Do not be concerned that there may be duplication of answers here compared to those above) | Values of Recognition, Financial Security, Being Wanted and Needed. The extrovert in me should energize me to try different ways of doing things. I have a low to moderate expressive and interpersonal communication preference style—this could be more emphasized to make the change happen. My parents would be proud to see that I could be successful and still be seen as a good person with healthy relationships. Do I really need to feel stressed and proving myself all the time? Some changes might make this feeling change for the better. I have a strength in helping people in bettering their knowledge but don't use this very often—the change would make that more of a continuing reality and I might be seen as a mentor. Could make the "culture" to "culture" connection amongst people more productive and lower conflict and frustrations and misunderstanding. *Note: Other personal private matters arose in these answers that are not reported above.* |
| **Fourth phase** | **Insights, commitments and actions** | |
| Step 11 | Reflection and insights: What deep **insights emerged for you** about your assumptions, influences, **drivers and blockers** across your answers in Steps 3–10? Summarize your insights here. How do these insights compare and contrast with any feedback you may have received? | A better balance of urgency and engaging people is likely to be better for the longer term. I can be results driven and a bit more feminine without appearing weak. It is possible to be self-confident, and still get value from other people's views. It does not have to be "either … or". I might be surprised with the ideas I get from others by asking more questions. There may be a way to have success in this sector without the stress of a burnout. I can always control how much attention I give. More thought about this is not that hard—just needs practice—and some feedback. I have to stop punishing myself and see some happiness. I'm carrying too many demons, and these are unhealthy—especially in my personal life. *Note: Further personal private matters arose in these answers that are not reported above.* |

(*continued*)

**Table 8.1** (continued)

| | Tool question | Jennifer's responses in going through the drivers and blockers surfacing methodology |
|---|---|---|
| Step 12 | Restated aspiration, development objective and commitments:<br>Take some time now to **reflect** on these **insights** and consider the **implications** for your own leadership development, as well as the actions you will need to take to achieve your development objective<br>Re-state your leadership aspiration and your development objective to include these insights, and propose your concrete actions for change (including experimentation) that **unleash your drivers and overcome your blockers**<br>Deeply reflect on your answers and make any further adjustments to ensure you have a clear, concrete and prioritized **commitment** for your future **leadership development and growth**<br>List the proposed key commitments and actions you will take to turn your development objective into reality, including how you will get support and feedback from others to help meet your development objective | I will have to make deep and active listening a priority if I want to effectively involve and interact with people—across different backgrounds and perspectives. This will demonstrate that I respond to feedback and can reduce stress levels and improve career prospects.<br>So, my updated **leadership vision and development objective with proposed action steps and support is:**<br>**I will be** the motivating leader of people want to be, and be highly recognized for my experience, results and knowledge. I will be seen as a business executive capable of leading the entire organization, not just my finance management area. A leader who can balance fairness with actions. A leader who can listen, engage and direct as needed. A leader who is seen as calm and controlled.<br>**Action steps and support commitments:**<br>Begin discussions with questions as the opening including follow up questions. Spend some moments preparing these before important discussions. Include practicing some personal chit-chat when meeting team members and increase level of question asking.<br>Will ask a lot more open questions rather than using statements in the question format. Will not be cutting people off and allowing them to finish and try to reduce interruptions and I should be monitoring my interruption levels. Attempting to make sure I have enough personal energy before going into important conversations where listening is needed—and this may drain me. Will seek direct feedback from peers and direct reports on these behaviors.<br>Will control my voice when I start to feel frustrated and try to keep my body calmer with both feet on the floor. Also use some deep breaths—or practice "time-outs". I will need to add some of the mindfulness techniques we've been looking at in the program including meditation. Will try to add some defined personal recovery time in my diary.<br>At meetings or in discussions, make a conscious choice as to whether to keep the phone on or switch it off and put it away at the beginning. Will keep a checklist to monitor this—and share this with my coach.<br>Will do some team development work where I can try out new behaviors. I think I need to find a female mentor who has managed this all better in the finance business.<br>I will make some changes in my personal life. *(These private matters are not reported here.)*<br>*(continued)* |

**Table 8.1** (continued)

| | Tool question | Jennifer's responses in going through the drivers and blockers surfacing methodology |
|---|---|---|
| Step 13 | Broader leadership context:<br>You could now turn to think about your **broader leadership work, activities and behaviors** beyond the specific development objective you were exploring.<br>Think about all your answers to Steps 7–10 where you uncovered **potential drivers in yourself**. In what other leadership situations or contexts could you make these a **very positive contributor**? Are there any potential leadership situations where these **drivers might become negative blockers?** | Being extrovert as a driver could energize me to get more socially involved with people.<br>By converting the knowledge and experience I have to some mentoring, I can try to take on some training of key talent. Could also consider reaching out to my old university and seeing if there a few talents for the future I might work with—particularly future female finance and accounting graduates.<br>Possible Blocks: Will need to be careful about this mentoring because I don't want to be seen as undermining the people below me by stepping over them to their juniors and jumping in to direct. Also, as I'm working to improve my listening skills, I need these to be much better to be a good mentor. May need to get others in our team involved in a project like this when I think I'm ready and delay this possible project with good planning. |
| Step 14 | Another reflection:<br>Think about all your answers to Steps 3–6 where **you uncovered potential blockers in yourself**. In what **different leadership situations or contexts** could you make these blockers become a **very positive contributor?** In effect, to turn these weaknesses into strengths? | A change to include the mentoring project could mean I help others avoid the blockers I thought about coming from my own professional experience in finance.<br>I could try to find some people in my next recruitments who are good at balancing the results with their people skills and have them help me and my team.<br>Could also have our team agree on some "rules" for mobile phones that we can all stick to—Or try to.<br>*Note: One personal and private matter arose here that is not reported.* |

[a]An example from our research (see Sect. 10.1, Example 40)

## 8.3 Integrating Drivers and Blockers Exploration with Leadership Development

As we noted in the opening Chap. 1, exploring drivers and blockers in and of itself does not constitute integrated leadership development—it is aimed at increasing profound self-awareness. To be meaningful, and actionable, such exploration should be part of a well-designed leadership development approach that includes feedback, reflection, practice and a support system—all assisting to help an individual progressively develop themselves and achieve transformational change.

By way of giving an example of this, we take one of the many integrated and holistic leadership development approaches, to see the way exploring drivers and blockers can enrich self-awareness and enliven, as well as enlighten, the development journey for an executive. This is the "Insightfully Aware Leadership Development Framework (IALD)".[1] Field research using the "Drivers and Blockers Exploration Tool" presented in this book also contributed to enhancements and continuing development of that framework itself.

In the IALD framework, leadership development is grounded on generating insights by examining self, in relation to others and context—with an intensive focus on understanding hidden "assumptions and influences, drivers and blockers". In this development journey, leaders will progressively gather and use profound insights about themselves, others and context to help guide and support leadership decisions, behaviors and development (Woodward & Shaffakat, 2016). The IALD incorporates persistent and dynamic insight generation, feedback, reflection, practice and action underpinning support throughout the different building blocks. The visual below (see Fig. 8.2) draws this together. Although the building blocks appear in sequence, the reality is that the steps and activities are interactive and interweaving—with a leader working simultaneously on their development in more than one block at any point in time and working to create their ecosystem of support.

The "Intensive Awareness: Exploring Drivers and Blockers" building block is a crucial and interlinked feature of this framework. The underlying rationale for the exercise that explores drivers and blockers as a discrete, yet intertwined, component is deepening continuous self-awareness

---

[1] Insightfully Aware Leadership Development Framework V3.1—Ian C Woodward—September 2017.

**Fig. 8.2** Insightfully aware leadership development framework (2017). (Published with kind permission of the author © I.C. Woodward (2017). All Rights Reserved)

as a dynamic part of integrated leadership development. An individual explores these directly related to his or her specific development objectives and context, to see what drivers he or she can use to support change; and what blockers might be standing in the way.

As we have argued throughout this book, we believe that insights from using an exploration process for uncovering drivers and blockers can act as an invaluable lens in increasing the depth of self-awareness. As such, it is a construct that should have wide applicability in leadership development programs, interventions and coaching.

CHAPTER 9

# Conclusion and Opportunities for Further Research and Application

*Everything that irritates us about others can lead us to an understanding of ourselves.*
Carl Gustav Jung

Since publication of Robert Kegan and Lisa Lahey's article "The Real Reason People Won't Change" in *Harvard Business Review* in 2001, there has been an explosion of interest in understanding the forces impeding people's change efforts. The breadth of research into the role of the conscious and unconscious mind in understanding the reasons for intrapersonal change is more limited, but we note that the relationship between conscious and unconscious is highlighted by many scholars. In our research, we examine these conscious and unconscious forces and their roles as drivers and blockers, employing the psychodynamic approach. Kegan & Lahey (2001a, 2009) focused on uncovering people's "competing commitments" and the related hidden assumptions that hinder their commitment to change. Our work is an extension and complementary to this, looking in detail into what these competing commitments and hidden assumptions (i.e. blockers) could be, as well as how similar or other factors can act as drivers in one's change and development efforts.

Our book adds to a growing body of literature that brings the intrapersonal domain to the center stage in developing leaders (Day, 2001; Mumford, Helton, Decker, Connelly, & Van Doorn, 2003; Shamir & Eilam, 2005). In particular, it extends previous studies on self-awareness, change behaviors and leadership development (e.g. Mayo et al., 2012; Petriglieri et al., 2011). Through an extensive literature review and specific field research examples, we direct readers to exemplars of leaders in different roles, experiencing difficulties in accomplishing their change objectives and overcoming these difficulties. We highlight the drivers and blockers, which are conscious or unconscious, operating in these examples. Drivers and blockers form the part of cognitive processing core to psychodynamics (Barsade et al., 2009). We hope that exploring drivers and blockers will open new areas for further research and pedagogical deployment.

We provided the "Drivers and Blockers Exploration Tool" and its surfacing and discovery process, based on our literature review and our leadership development research, practice and experience, to assist leaders or executives in bringing about their desired transformation. Such an exploration would be a part of an integrated approach to generating profound insights within a comprehensive leadership development process, understanding and examining one's self in relation to others and context, marked by an enhanced focus on considering and reflecting on drivers and blockers operating within us. The "Drivers and Blockers Exploration Tool" is an extension and evolution of Kegan & Lahey's (2009) "four-column exercise" on "immunity to change", Boyatzis's (2006) "Intentional Change Theory" and the range of integrated leadership development approaches discussed in the opening chapters.

Further research, we believe, could uncover relevant aspects given less attention in the literature. For example, in our Chaps. 6 and 7 discussions, we highlighted a research opportunity to look at whether the different reservoirs of drivers and blockers may be interrelated, or interdependent. We also noted the research potential for examining behavioral patterns (such as Alpha/Beta) as reflectors of drivers and/or blockers.

Participant observation (e.g. Lofland & Lofland, 2006) could offer insights into the way transformation manifests in practice for executives and provide contextually richer data in relation to drivers and blockers. It would be interesting to observe how elements of national culture (ethnicity) hinder or promote a leader's development efforts, where developmental objectives are determined from a culturally different perspective to the executive's background. Studies have highlighted the role of these factors on people's emotions (Bagozzi, Verbeke, & Gavino, 2003); the way they deal with power dynamics (Mondillon et al., 2005); the way they deal with change in general (Oreg et al., 2008) and also on leadership ratings

(Atwater, Wang, Smither, & Fleenor, 2009). Research on the role of gender could also examine whether patterns exist among men and women with regard to their particular drivers and blockers. Future research could also look into the role of hierarchical levels in shaping drivers and blockers. In addition, longitudinal studies could examine leaders' experiences of change development with regular exploration of the same development objective as attempted over time.

Also, longitudinal studies with variable-interval schedules (Iida, Shrout, Laurenceau, & Bolger, 2012) could be used in further research on drivers and blockers. Longitudinal studies could be more suitable for understanding an individual's experiences over a period of time and how these vary from one individual to another with regard to specific drivers and blockers. Longitudinal studies can also determine what process underlies an individual's change and development and how individuals vary in this process, making them particularly appropriate for drivers and blockers research. Future research could also explore the relationships between mini-selves (Bachkirova, 2011) and identity theory (Stets & Burke, 2000) as well as how drivers and blockers relate to cognitive sources of bias in behavioral decision theory (Schwenk, 1986). Another future study arena signaled in Chap. 6 is the question of life experiences influencing the sources of drivers and blockers. A large amount of literature connects life experiences and "nurture" to many areas of the reservoirs (e.g. some personality and trait aspects, as well as values and motivators). However, there is only very limited research that analyzes the connection between these life experiences, and the specific driver and/or blocker that assist or work against a particular leadership development objective (such as increasing active listening or reducing micro-management).

The potential application of exploring drivers and blockers could be examined comprehensively at team and organizational levels in future research. This presents a rich area for examination, as the times when we have undertaken the exploration exercise with whole leadership teams have yielded very powerful insights for group discussion. This has frequently led to discussion items on organizational culture and values, as well as the role model behaviors (positive and negative) on display from members of the leadership team.

While our early results are very encouraging, there will need to be continuous testing, evaluation and research on the application and refinement of the "Drivers and Blockers Exploration Tool", which will be the subject of future studies, published research and commentary. Its application in senior executive education programs and coaching will help understand its pedagogical efficacy in terms of enhancing the programs' reflective and personalization components. It may provide further insights into how leaders develop in executive courses grounded in a "clinical" approach (Kets de Vries & Korotov, 2007; Wood & Petriglieri, 2005), supporting scholarship on immersive leadership programs that involve coaching, action learning, 360-degree leadership assessment, case exercises and personalization (Boyatzis, Stubbs, & Taylor, 2002; Hoover, Giambatista, Sorenson, & Bommer, 2010; Petriglieri et al., 2011).

With this book as the outcome of our research and practice, we hope to draw the attention of academics, executive educators, coaches and leaders to the importance and potential benefits of exploring drivers and blockers. As committed leadership development professionals and academics, we have seen the tremendous value of deepening levels of insightful awareness when leaders uncover their hidden assumptions and forces, unleash their drivers and overcome their blockers to help make the change they want a reality.

## 9.1 Afterword: Drivers and Blockers: A Final Reflection

> The bad poet is usually unconscious where he ought to be conscious, and conscious where he ought to be unconscious. (T. S. Eliot)

As a final reflection and afterword, we chose some poetry to reflect on the potential importance of discovering one's drivers and blockers in all of us.

One poem that holds much leadership meaning is by the British poet William Ernest Henley (1849–1903). It is the poem "Invictus" written in 1875 and published in 1888. This poem was read regularly by Nelson Mandela during his many years in prison to remember personal courage; and was given by Mandela, as President, to the Captain of the Springbok Rugby team for inspiration in the 1995 World Cup. There are illusions to drivers and blockers throughout these words:

> *Out of the night that covers me,*
> *Black as the pit from pole to pole,*
> *I thank whatever gods may be*
> *For my unconquerable soul.*

> *In the fell clutch of circumstance*
> *I have not winced nor cried aloud.*
> *Under the bludgeonings of chance*
> *My head is bloody, but unbowed.*
> *Beyond this place of wrath and tears*
> *Looms but the horror of the shade,*
> *And yet the menace of the years*
> *Finds, and shall find me, unafraid.*
> *It matters not how strait the gate,*
> *How charged with punishments the scroll,*
> *I am the master of my fate:*
> *I am the captain of my soul.*

Source: Public Domain. See for example, https://www.poets.org/poets-org/poem/invictus

Another very thoughtful work comes from the distinguished contemporary British poet, William Ayot, in his poetry book *E-mail from the Soul*. The poem was written for business executive undertaking leadership development, and is entitled "You Guys":

> *This is your time*
> *For frosty mornings in towns you will never know,*
> *For resentful receptionists and chirpy secretaries,*
> *For flipcharts and outcomes, for plans and reports,*
> *For too much coffee and too many words.*
> *This is your time.*
> *This is your time*
> *For dressing in the dark and cars to the airport.*
> *For planes and trains and railway stations;*
> *For loneliness, for grief, for embracing doubt,*
> *For keeping hard secrets in the face of love.*
> *This is your time.*
> *This is your time*
> *For being what your people need you to be,*
> *For managing fear while showing calm,*
> *For being their mother, for being their father,*
> *For holding the line, or the hope, or the dream.*
> *This is your time.*
> *This is your time*
> *For sudden sunlight breaking through the overcast,*
> *For sweet green spaces in concrete canyons;*

*For the care of strangers, for anonymous gifts,*
*For learning to receive little acts of kindness.*
*This is your time.*
*This is your time*
*For standing to be counted, for being yourself,*
*For becoming the sum and total of your life,*
*For finding courage, for finding your voice,*
*For leading, because you are needed now.*
*This is your time.*

Published with kind permission of the author © William Ayot (2013). All Rights Reserved. "You Guys" is found in the book 'E-mail from the Soul: New & Selected Leadership Poems' by William Ayot. Publisher PS Avalon, Glastonbury, 2013.

# CHAPTER 10

# Appendices

## 10.1 Appendix 1: List of Participant Field Research Examples Demonstrating Drivers and Blockers

|   | Name | Designation | Industry | Driver | Blocker |
|---|------|-------------|----------|--------|---------|
| **Competing commitment and "big assumption"** | | | | | |
| 1 | Lorenz | Business head | Automotive | To be a leader who promotes growth environment by empowering team members | "Assumption" that only tight control would ensure quality results |
| **Possible-selves** | | | | | |
| 2 | Takashi | General manager | Professional services | Focused, positive possible self as a CEO in the future | Self-view of not being good at team work and people-oriented skills in general |
| **World views** | | | | | |
| 3 | Steve | Director | Energy | | Ontological Perceptual Constraint—"my way is the optimum way" |

(*continued*)

|   | Name | Designation | Industry | Driver | Blocker |
|---|---|---|---|---|---|
| 4 | Andrew | Senior executive | Consumer goods | | Ontological Functional Constraint—"compromise" shows "weakness and lack of leadership" |
| **Emotions** | | | | | |
| 5 | Aaron | Business head | Banking/financial services | | Fear of becoming less business oriented |
| 6 | Emma | Seasoned executive | Banking/financial services | Feeling proud for managing her time well, and feeling confident taking the right decisions | Feelings of becoming "unapproachable" and being perceived as "proud and arrogant" |
| **Personality traits** | | | | | |
| 7 | Emma[a] | Seasoned executive | Banking/financial services | | High agreeableness |
| 8 | Alex | Associate | Professional services | High agreeableness | |
| 9 | Kenneth | Banking executive | Banking/financial services | | Low agreeableness |
| 10 | Ali | Physician | Health services | Low agreeableness | |
| 11 | Martin | General manager | Consumer goods | | Introversion |
| 12 | Thomas | Executive | Energy | Introversion | |
| 13 | John | Business head | Banking/financial services | | Extraversion |
| 14 | Fred | Operations executive | Banking/financial services | Extraversion | |
| 15 | Laurel | Manager | Technology | | High conscientiousness |
| 16 | Fred[a] | Operations executive | Banking/financial services | High conscientiousness | |
| 17 | Richard | Case writer | Higher education | | Low conscientiousness |

|    | Name | Designation | Industry | Driver | Blocker |
|----|------|-------------|----------|--------|---------|
| 18 | Christina | System analyst | Technology | Low conscientiousness | |
| 19 | Mary | Administrative staff member | Education | High neuroticism | High neuroticism |
| 20 | Peter | Investment banker | Banking/financial services | | Low neuroticism |
| 21 | Victor | Senior project Lead | Construction | Low neuroticism | |
| 22 | Laurel[a] | Manager | Technology | | Less open to experience |
| 23 | Kathy | Senior operations executive | Logistics and supply chain management | Less open to experience | |
| 24 | Greg | Senior sales executive | Machinery and equipment industry | | Highly open to experience |
| 25 | Mark | Writer | | Highly open to experience | |
| 26 | Fred[a] | Operations executive | Banking/financial services | High self-esteem | |
| 27 | Roger | Senior executive | Energy | | Low self-esteem |
| 28 | Barbara | Manager | Consumer goods Company | | External locus of control |
| 29 | Shirley | Senior lecturer | Higher education | | Risk aversion |
| 30 | Laurel[a] | Manager | Technology | | Low tolerance for ambiguity |
| **Other examples** | | | | | |
| 31 | Adriano | Divisional CEO | Media | | Negative self-esteem |
| 32 | Sylvia | Divisional head | Health services | Positive self-efficacy | |
| 33 | Thomas[a] | Executive | Energy | Positive emotional engagement | |
| 34 | Roger[a] | Senior executive | Energy | | Self-esteem struggles |
| **Values** | | | | | |
| 35 | Martin[a] | General manager | Consumer goods | Recognition, achievement | Integrity, transparency |

*(continued)*

| Name | Designation | Industry | Driver | Blocker |
|---|---|---|---|---|
| 36 Emma[a] | Seasoned executive | Banking/financial services | Inner peace, honesty, respect | Self-fulfillment, caring about others, being generous |
| **Extrinsic and intrinsic motivators** | | | | |
| 37 Andrew[a] | Senior executive | Consumer company | Recognition (extrinsic-positive motivation) | Fear of being perceived as weak (extrinsic-negative motivation) |
| | | | Achievement (intrinsic-positive motivator) | Fear of not being in control (intrinsic-negative motivation) |
| **The "drivers and blockers exploration tool" mini cases** | | | | |
| 38 Stefanie | Chief Operating Officer | Energy company | *Development objective explored: ineffective leadership communication and engagement* See complete answers in Sect. 10.8 | *Development objective explored: ineffective leadership communication and engagement* See complete answers in Sect. 10.8 |
| 39 Markus | Chief Executive Officer | Consumer goods company | *Development objective explored: domineering control and micro-management* See complete answers in Sect. 10.8 | *Development objective explored: domineering control and micro-management* See complete answers in Sect. 10.8 |
| 40 Jennifer | Chief Financial Officer | Specialist financial services firm | *Development objective explored: lack of active listening with impatience in interactions with others* See complete answers in Chap. 8 | *Development objective explored: lack of active listening with impatience in interactions with others* See complete answers in Chap. 8 |

|    | Name | Designation | Industry | Driver | Blocker |
|----|------|-------------|----------|--------|---------|
| 41 | John | Chief Operating Officer | Transportation company | *Development objective explored: lack of assertiveness* See complete answers in Sect. 10.8 | *Development objective explored: lack of assertiveness* See complete answers in Sect. 10.8 |
| **Drivers and blockers overview example** | | | | | |
| 42 | Olivia | Marketing Director | Retail services | *Development objective explored: overly dominating discussions and conversations—too much "air time"* See Chap. 1 major example | *Development objective explored: overly dominating discussions and conversations—too much "air time"* See Chap. 1 major example |

All these field research examples were participants selected from more than 2000 global executives who were enrolled in different leadership development programs or participants in coaching or training interventions with the authors between years 2013 and 2018. The cited examples are from responses where drivers and blockers exploration was undertaken. To protect confidentiality and anonymity, the real names and identifying information of all the participants have not been used with all private information disguised.

[a]Participant examples used multiple times in the book

## 10.2  Appendix 2: "Orders of Mind" (Adapted from Kegan, 1994 and Additional Sources as Cited)

| Order of mind | 3rd order: "the socialized mind" | 4th order: "the self-authoring mind" | 5th order: "self-transforming mind" |
|---|---|---|---|
| Description | Socialized mind individuals are:<br>  Strongly influenced by other people's perspectives, opinions and expectations, which thereby censor their words and actions (Kegan & Lahey, 2009)<br>  They tend to be good team players (Kegan & Lahey, 2009)<br>  They hold internalized sense of mutuality in interpersonal associations and are therefore accountable for their own function in the wider community (Berger, Hasegawa, Hammerman, & Kegan, 2007) | Self-authoring mind individuals are:<br>  Self-directed and self-assured individuals who tend to have strong beliefs and are strongly committed to those beliefs (Kegan & Lahey, 2009)<br>  They have a focus, a plan, a stance, an approach, an evaluation of what is required (Kegan & Lahey, 2009)<br>  They can recognize various intrinsic aspects of themselves that might be interacting with one another and can take accountability for their intrinsic states and emotions (Berger et al., 2007) | Self-transforming mind individuals<br>  Take a step back from their own frame and "look at it", not simply "through it" (Kegan & Lahey, 2009, p. 19)<br>  Critically assess their own ideologies and "re-author a more comprehensive view" as required when the information they seek suggests an alteration in outlook to fit the constantly evolving environment (Kegan & Lahey, 2009, p. 25)<br>  Show increased levels of work-competence (Kegan & Lahey, 2009)<br>  Endorse transformation at different levels, individual, team and organizational (Rooke & Torbert, 1998; Torbert, 2006) |

| Order of mind | 3rd order: "the socialized mind" | 4th order: "the self-authoring mind" | 5th order: "self-transforming mind" |
| --- | --- | --- | --- |
| Potential limitations of this order of mind | Have difficulty making a decision when faced with conflict between important beliefs, individuals or institutions<br>Can lead to group-think, where team member can conceal important pieces of information from decision processes so as to avoid conflict and maintain unanimity (Kegan & Lahey, 2009) | Have trouble identifying or spotting flaws with their beliefs<br>Look for ideas that match their mind frames thereby neglecting ones that do not<br>Struggle with shifts in environment, in terms of detecting the changes, reviewing the situation and changing their approach (Kegan & Lahey, 2009) | Can hold exaggerated sense of satisfaction with oneself which can lead to over-confidence and under-estimation of risks |
| Stage of ego development | 'Unformed ego'-implies<br>    Unsatisfied needs; and<br>    Unaccomplished tasks (Bachkirova, 2011) | 'Formed ego'- (fulfilling stage) marked by<br>    Accomplishment; and<br>    Freedom (Bachkirova, 2011) | 'Reformed ego'- Characterizes a more compatible association between the conscious and unconscious mind reflected in an individual's capacity to stand the uncertainty of certain needs and tasks<br>    Marked by an increased awareness of the nature of the information that brain and mind intake (Bachkirova, 2011) |
| Level of self awareness | Medium | High | Exceptional |

*(continued)*

| Order of mind | 3rd order: "the socialized mind" | 4th order: "the self-authoring mind" | 5th order: "self-transforming mind" |
| --- | --- | --- | --- |
| Examples of communication approaches | With a socialized mind, an individual communicates, what he/she believes others want to hear (Kegan & Lahey, 2009) | With a self-authoring mind, an individual communicates, what he/she believes is essential for others to hear so as to advance his/her plan of work (Kegan & Lahey, 2009) | When self-transforming mind individuals communicate, they are not simply furthering their plan and approach but also creating an opportunity for adjusting and enhancing their plan or approach. With the self-transforming mind, one is inquiring and at the same time requesting for information (Kegan & Lahey, 2009) |

## 10.3 Appendix 3: Overcoming Immunity to Change—Kegan and Lahey's (2009) Four Column "Immunity Map"—Information Overview

According to Kegan and Lahey (2009), confronting adaptive problems such as immunity to change necessitates "an adaptive formulation of the problem" (i.e. a need to see how the problem stands with regards to the potential of one's mental complexity) and "an adaptive solution" (i.e. a need to adapt oneself in certain ways) (p. 31). The former is not just about cognition; instead, it is a combination of one's thinking and one's emotions. Adaptive formulation needs to provide the individual with a different, novel way of analyzing and interpreting than they have had previously. This can immediately give the person insights; at the same exposing the "emotional ecology" that lies at the root of the problem (p. 31). The adaptive formulation or the specific illustration of the immunity to change gives an image of how an individual is fighting against his/her genuine commitments in an orderly fashion. Adaptive formulation entails drawing a mental map which works like an X-ray, "a picture of invisible made visible" (Kegan & Lahey, 2009, p. 32). This

X-ray or the "immunity map" enables people to see not just the current state of situation but also why it is the way it is, and what needs to be changed to get meaningful and novel outcomes.

Adaptive formulation or creating an image of one's immune system (specifically uncovering one's own competing commitments) makes it easier to work on the immune system rather than being trapped by it. Adaptive formulation or understanding how one's self-protective motivations impede people from achieving the change they are sincerely committed to is important. However, these insights, though effective, might not result in transformation (Kegan & Lahey, 2009). According to Kegan and Lahey (2001b), most individuals will require a structure to enable them to direct their desires, check and detach themselves from their "assumptions" and slowly create new techniques to connect their intentions and behaviors. Kegan and Lahey (2001b) therefore, provide a sequence of steps which can be helpful in overturning immunities (Wagner et al., 2006). These steps include:

- Design the metrics to identify costs and progress
- Observe the Big Assumption in action
- Stay alert to challenges to the Big Assumption
- Write the biography of the Big Assumption
- Design a test of your Big Assumption
- Run the test
- Develop new designs and new tests

The first step involves delineating the goals of the person's immunity to change and constructing an image of what it would be like to overcome one's competing commitments. This image will act as a motivator for people to engage in this endeavor. The aim here is to set a context to attempt changes, which will with time become clearer. Furthermore, this step also involves evaluation of the existing costs to an individual if he or she maintains the status quo. The purpose of this step is to remind an individual of the necessity of making the change and disturbing the immune system (Wagner et al., 2006).

The purpose of the second step is to be aware of the situations where one can observe one's "assumption" in action, such as how one views entities, perceives them, decides, acts and uses one's energy (Wagner et al., 2006). After observing the "Big Assumption" at work, one needs to be vigilant and look for situations that question the validity of these "assumptions", which is the third step (Wagner et al., 2006). The fourth step involves examining the 'record' of one's "assumptions", how did they come into existence and how long has an individual being living with them (Wagner et al., 2006).

The fifth step involves coming up with a test to evaluate one's "Big Assumption" as a way to prepare, before formally testing one's "Big Assumption" (Wagner et al., 2006). The sixth step involves going forward with the test and keeping track of the events as they unfold. The aim here is to check the consequences of altering or changing one's usual approach, followed by a reflection on the results with regards to the "Big Assumption" identified (Wagner et al., 2006).

In the last step, if the results of one's first test were positive, one will have useful feedback on the "Big Assumption", which can then be treated as hypotheses on varied ways of one's functioning. In the subsequent tests, one can test these hypotheses, coupled with different behaviors resulting in additional hypotheses. Eventually the ones that produce good results can translate into "assumptions" that can steer one's behavior (Wagner et al., 2006). These steps reflect a sequence which demonstrates the basic process of overturning a person's immunities.

In process of working through Kegan and Lahey's (2009) discovery of immunity to change and competing commitments, this is often undertaken in coaching and development activities by working across four columns:

1. The Commitment and Description of the Change Desired
2. A List of what the Person is Doing/Not Doing Preventing the Change
3. Examine the Hidden Commitments (sometimes fears) related to the current behaviors identified in (2), and
4. Big Assumptions (the reasons) behind and underneath the Hidden Commitments identified in (3)

## 10.4  Appendix 4: System 1 and System 2—Automatic and Controlled Mind

| System 1 (automatic & intuitive) | System 2 (controlled & reflective) |
| --- | --- |
| Process characteristics | |
| Automatic | Controlled |
| Effortless | Effortful |
| Associative | Deductive |
| Rapid, parallel | Slow, serial |
| Process opaque | Self-aware |
| Skilled action | Rule application |
| Content on which processes act | |
| Affective | Neutral |
| Causal propensities | Statistics |
| Concrete, specific | Abstract |
| Prototypes | Sets |

Adapted and combined from Kahneman & Frederick (2002); and Kahneman (2011)

## 10.5  Appendix 5: Comparing Five Factor NEO-P (Big Five) with MBTI

| The five factor NEO-PI[a] (Costa & McCrae, 1985) | The Myers-Briggs type indicator (Myers & McCaulley, 1985) |
| --- | --- |
| Features | |
| Self-administered/self report (Costa & McCrae, 1985) | Self-administered/self-report (Myers & McCaulley, 1985) |
| Based on the Big Five (openness, conscientiousness, extraversion, agreeableness, and neuroticism) | Based on Jung's theory of personality types (extraversion–introversion; thinking–feeling, sensation–intuition, and judging–perceiving) (Myers & McCaulley, 1985) |
| Five Factor Model (FFM) of personality (Costa & McCrae, 1985) | |
| Refers to personality traits (Costa & McCrae, 1985) | Refers to personality types (Myers & McCaulley, 1985) |
| Comprised of 240 items (statements), rating through 5-point Likert scale (Costa & McCrae, 1985) | Contains 94 choice items that make up four bipolar discontinuous scales |
| | A total of 16 personality type profiles produced (Myers & McCaulley, 1985) |
| Responses are coded and analyzed to get facet scores (Costa & McCrae, 1985) | Respondents are ascribed to 1 of the 16 personality types as per the score they get for each scale (Myers & McCaulley, 1985) |

(*continued*)

| The five factor NEO-PI[a] (Costa & McCrae, 1985) | The Myers-Briggs type indicator (Myers & McCaulley, 1985) |
|---|---|
| Common in academia (Carskadon, 1979; Davito, 1985) | Common in counseling and management (Carskadon, 1979; Davito, 1985) |
| **Criticism** | |
| Derived from factor-analytic work, certain dimensions of which are methodically flawed (Boyle & Saklofske, 2004) | Missing emotional stability/ neuroticism dimension (McCrae & Costa, 1989) |
| Construct validity of FFM has been doubted despite its wide acceptance (Boyle, 1997; Boyle, Stankov, & Cattell, 1995; Eysenck, 1992; Heather, 1995) | No bimodal distribution of preference scores (Furnham, 1996) |
| Gives a "static" description of personality (Terracciano, Costa, & McCrae, 2006). However research suggests that constant changes to personality structure take place throughout life (Cattell, Boyle, & Chant, 2002; Fraley & Roberts, 2005) | Does not support the Jungian theory (Hicks, 1984; Stricker & Ross, 1964) or validate the measures (Saggino, Cooper, & Kline, 1999) |
| **Convergence between MBTI and four of the Big Five dimensions** | |
| McCrae & Costa (1989) | |
| Extraversion is correlated to → | Extraversion-introversion |
| Openness to experience is correlated to → | Sensing-intuition |
| Agreeableness is correlated to → | Thinking-feeling |
| Conscientiousness is correlated to → | Judging-perceiving |
| Furnham (1996) | |
| Agreeableness is correlated to → | Thinking-feeling |
| Conscientiousness is correlated to → | Judging-perceiving |
| Extraversion is correlated to → | Extraversion-introversion |
| Neuroticism is weakly related to → | Extraversion-introversion, thinking-feeling (overall inconsistent results) |
| Openness to experience is correlated to → | Sensing-intuition |
| Tobacyk, Livingston, & Robbins (2008) | |
| Extraversion is correlated to → | Extraversion-introversion |
| Openness to experience is correlated to → | Judging-perceiving |
| Openness to experience is correlated to → | Sensing-intuition |
| Conscientiousness is correlated to → | Judging-perceiving |
| Agreeableness is weakly related to → | Thinking-feeling |

[a] A revised version of NEO PI is referred to as NEO PI-R, which includes six specific facets within each of the five domains (Berry et al., 2001)

## 10.6 APPENDIX 6: SUMMARY DESCRIPTION OF VARIOUS RESERVOIRS AND SOURCES OF DRIVERS AND BLOCKERS

| Sources | Description | Driver | Blocker |
|---|---|---|---|
| Conscious processes | Processes that require intentional and deliberate engagement of conscious thought (Kahneman, 2011) | Can help us make rational decision by viewing things in totality, especially based on feedback | Can be overpowered by unconscious |
| Unconscious and automatic processes | Processes that are fast, effective and not in the domain of conscious thereby lacking forethought and consideration (Kahneman, 2011) | May be sufficient to make us pursue a goal with no conscious awareness needed | Can draw away energy from the change process |
| Mini-selves | A pattern of associations between various points of the brain that are activated or inhibited when an individual performs an action (Bachkirova, 2011) | Can act as drivers if they are complementary or if there is coordination and communication between them | Can act as blockers performing their individual roles as suits them and may even fulfill the needs, which then conflict with one another |
| Possible-selves | "Cognitive manifestation of enduring goals, aspirations, motives, fears, threats" (Markus & Nurius, 1986, p. 158). They are the selves we wish to become as positive aspirations (e.g. prosperous self, famous self, highly regarded self) or fear becoming (e.g. incapable self, solitary self, addict-self) (Markus & Nurius, 1986) | Can act as drivers by enabling individuals to model essential strategies for achieving their goals | Can act as blockers expressed as people's fears or worries, demotivating them and preventing them from taking steps to achieve their objectives |

*(continued)*

| Sources | Description | Driver | Blocker |
| --- | --- | --- | --- |
| Worldviews | Include "beliefs, assumptions, attitudes, values and ideas to form a comprehensive model of reality....encompass formulations and interpretations of past, present and future" (Schlitz, Vieten, & Miller, 2010, p. 19) | Can help individuals understand the implications of change, especially when the change is positive and thereby help them know where they are heading | Might not adequately explain what is viewed and experienced. Being embedded and becoming subliminal, with time they can act as blockers |
| Emotions | "An organized and highly structured reaction to an event that is relevant to the needs, goals or survival of an organism" (Watson & Clark, 1994b, p. 89) | Can act as drivers, by managing, stimulating and helping people achieve what is needed. Certain emotions motivate individuals to embrace adaptive behaviors | Negative emotions can act as blockers, enabling people to form numerous intrinsic defense mechanisms that surface automatically as a reaction to the *feelings* of psychological threat and are endorsed by individuals to mitigate negative *emotions* |
| Personality and traits | "An individual's characteristic patterns of thought, emotion and behavior, together with the psychological mechanisms—hidden or not behind those patterns" (Funder, 1997, pp. 1–2) | | |
| "Big Five" | Include dimensions of openness to experience, conscientiousness, extraversion, agreeableness, and neuroticism (McCrae & Costa, 1986) | Can encourage individuals to direct, or accept change (see Table 5.1 for details) | Can encourage individuals to oppose change (see Table 5.1 for details) |

| Sources | Description | Driver | Blocker |
|---|---|---|---|
| Self-esteem | A universal dispositional feature related to an overall perception of self-efficacy and worth (Judge, Thoresen, et al., 1999) | High self-esteem, when under check, can act as a driver in one's change efforts. In research, high self-esteem is associated with a number of positive behaviors such as persistence at challenging jobs (Shrauger & Rosenberg, 1970), satisfaction (Diener, 1984), less neuroticism (Robins et al., 2001) | Self-esteem is marked with likelihood for misrepresentation (Claxton, 1994; Dunning, 2006) and numerous studies show various ways we may protect ourselves from attacks to our self-assessment (Fingarette, 2000; Goleman, 1997) Low self-esteem can act as a blocker making us perceive change as a threat and evoking resistance behaviors |
| Locus of control | Refers to one's beliefs of one's capacity to apply control over the context (Rotter, 1966) | Having a more internal locus of control enables people to better manage unfavorable environmental influences (Callan et al., 1994). Having an internal locus of control can act as a strong driver—a motivator—enabling an individual to apply more effort in making the change or achieving his or her objective | With an external locus of control, the drive to initiate change takes a back seat to influences that are seen to be beyond one's control. As such, individuals with an internal locus of control are less likely to be motivated to make an effort to produce the change |

*(continued)*

| Sources | Description | Driver | Blocker |
| --- | --- | --- | --- |
| Self-efficacy | Refers to "belief in one's capabilities to organize and execute the courses of action required to produce given attainment" (Bandura, 1997, p. 3) | Draws in a "mobilization or motivational component" that enables the adjustment of behavior to match changing situations (Gist & Mitchell, 1992). People with high self-efficacy are more likely to be optimistic about their commitments to tasks or change challenges | Lower levels of self-efficacy are associated with "defensive behavior", for example, resistance or protecting turf (Ashforth & Lee, 1990). People with lower levels of self-efficacy are more likely to feel less confident of their own ability to make the change |
| Positive affectivity | A key personality disposition mainly demonstrated in features such as optimism, confidence, enthusiasm, well-being and affiliation (Judge, Thoresen, et al., 1999) | People with high positive affectivity levels will be inclined to look for ways to proactively change for betterment (Duffy et al., 1998). Thus, positive affectivity can act as a driver in one's change efforts | |
| Negative affectivity | A key personality characteristic manifested in attributes such as negative emotional states (Kaplan et al., 2009; Watson & Clark, 1984) | | Negative affectivity meddles with the thinking needed for achieving goals and objectives (Frisch, 2006) and involves an individual's tendency to concentrate on negative aspects (Bowman & Stern, 1995; Penney & Spector, 2005). Negative affectivity can act as a blocker in an individual's change efforts |

| Sources | Description | Driver | Blocker |
|---|---|---|---|
| Tolerance for ambiguity | Can be regarded as a propensity to see ambiguous circumstances as desirable. On the contrary, intolerance of ambiguity connotes that the encounter with ambiguity is threatening (Budner, 1962) | Individuals with a high tolerance for ambiguity can deal with novel and ambiguous situations with less difficulty in comparison to ones with low tolerance for ambiguity (Barringer, 2008). High tolerance for ambiguity can, therefore, operate as a driver in one's change efforts | With the uncertainty, anxiety and stress associated with change, low tolerance for ambiguity is likely to act as a blocker in an individual's attempt to change |
| Risk aversion | Refers to the tendency of people to look for (risk-seeking) or keep away from risky situations (Kahneman & Tversky, 1979) | Willingness to take risks (risk-seeking) may impact the probability that individuals are more likely to explore options and initiate change perceived as upsetting the status quo, which might act as a driver, especially when change is important | Risk averse individuals are less likely to take chances and are more likely to get distressed in situations where risk was prominent (Cable & Judge, 1994; Judge, Thoresen, et al., 1999). Individuals who are risk-averse might view new and risk-related situations negatively. For them, risk aversion can act as a blocker |

(*continued*)

| Sources | Description | Driver | Blocker |
|---|---|---|---|
| Values | Are the "fundamental principles or standards—the essential elements of an individual, which guide his or her thinking, emotions, behaviors, actions and choices over time, and across multiple situations" (Woodward & Shaffakat, 2014, p. 21) | Values can influence our choice of a number of objectives as well as their achievement, though, maybe not directly. They can act as drivers for the objectives that relate to one's needs and aspirations | Values exist in our conscious and unconscious, and create both desires and fears (Woodward & Shaffakat, 2014). Conflicting values is one of the causes of resistance behaviors (Hultman, 2006; Wade, 1996; Williams, 2011) acting as a blocker in one's change efforts |
| Extrinsic and intrinsic motivators | Intrinsic motivation stems from an individual and is linked to efficiency and self-actualization, and extrinsic motivation originates from external factors and is associated with social reward (Herzberg 1959; Ryan & Deci, 2000) | The intrinsic-positive motivation, where the motivation stems from the sense of strength and security, and the extrinsic-positive motivation, where the motivation stems from recognition and acknowledgement can act as drivers in one's change efforts | Intrinsic-negative or extrinsic-negative motivation, which include threat, anxiety, insecurity and so on can act as potential blockers, which can impede our efforts in making the change |

## 10.7 Appendix 7: Drivers and Blockers Exploration Tool for Use and Adaptation

| | **First phase: Leadership aspiration and specific development objective** |
|---|---|
| Step 1 | Briefly state your overall **Leadership Aspiration** (or vision) for yourself as a leader into the future to be the "best leader you could be" |
| | |
| Step 2 | State **one** specific **development objective** for change in yourself. Also, state your **rationale** for making this change in your leadership behaviors. Then, briefly explain how succeeding in this objective will help you achieve your leadership aspiration. Be explicit and focused in stating this development objective or goal rather than being too general. (e.g. "Deep active listening" rather than "more emotionally intelligent" or "becoming a better leader") |
| | |
| | **Second phase: Exploring your Blockers** |
| Step 3 | List down the **current specific behaviors** that you are doing that are preventing you from achieving your personal leadership development objective stated in Step 2. This list might include behaviors or actions that you are not doing, that are contributing to your problem or issue<br><br>Next, for each current specific item in your list, put the **completely opposite behavior** for this in brackets next to each item |
| | |

**Fig. 10.1** Drivers and blockers exploration tool (2018 version) (The "Drivers and Blockers Exploration Tool" (2018) is published with kind permission of the authors © I.C. Woodward, S. Shaffakat and V.H. Dominé (2018). All Rights Reserved. The authors also provide that this tool may be copied or disseminated with source attribution, citation and acknowledgement for legitimate use by leadership development researchers and practitioners)

| | |
|---|---|
| Step 4 | Look at the list of **completely opposite behaviors** you described in Step 3. Imagine that you are now behaving in this completely opposite way<br><br>Do you have any **concerns, fears, worries, anxieties** or any other **negative emotions, feelings or thoughts**, if you imagine yourself behaving in these completely opposite ways? If so, what are these concerns and fears? |
| | |
| Step 5 | What **reasons** do you have, or **what assumptions** are you making for yourself, that could explain your negative concerns, feelings or fears identified in Step 4? |
| | |
| Step 6 | Carefully consider your answers to Step 5. Think about your **personal characteristics (such as personality, values, beliefs, attitudes, motivations); as well as your professional and personal life experiences.** Which of these characteristics and/or experiences would explain or underpin your **reasons and assumptions** answered in Step 5? (Do not be concerned that there may be duplication of answers here compared to those above.) |
| | |
| | **Third phase: Exploring your drivers** |
| Step 7 | Imagine you absolutely achieved your development objective stated in Step 2. Describe the **new or changed behaviors** you would be exhibiting. (These would be similar to those opposite behaviors you described to yourself in step 3 — but are now a much **more realistic list of behaviors**, rather than completely opposite behaviors.) |
| | |

**Fig. 10.1** Continued

| | |
|---|---|
| Step 8 | Reflect upon the new or changed behaviors you described in Step 7. What are the **positive emotions, feelings or thoughts** you are likely to have, or the **benefits** you might derive or see, if you achieve this change or behave in these new ways |
| | |
| Step 9 | What **reasons** do you have, or what **assumptions** are you making that could explain your positive feelings or the potential benefits identified in Step 8? |
| | |
| Step 10 | Carefully consider your answers to Step 9. Think about your **personal characteristics (such as personality, values, beliefs, attitudes, motivations); as well as your professional and personal life experiences.** Also think about your own **strengths and talents.** Which of these characteristics and/or experiences and/or strengths would explain or underpin your **reasons and assumptions** answered in Step 9? (Do not be concerned that there may be duplication of answers here compared to those above.) |
| | |

**Fig. 10.1** Continued

| | Fourth phase: Insights, commitments and actions |
|---|---|
| Step 11 | **Reflection and insights:**<br>What deep **insights emerged for you** about your assumptions, influences, **drivers and blockers** across your answers in Steps 3 to 10? Summarize your insights here. How do these insights compare and contrast with any feedback you may have received? |
| | |
| Step 12 | **Restated aspiration, development objective and commitments:**<br>Take some time now to **reflect** on these **insights** and consider the **implications** for your own leadership development, as well as the actions you will need to take to achieve your development objective<br><br>Re-state your leadership aspiration and your development objective to include these insights, and propose your concrete actions for change (including experimentation) that **unleash your drivers and overcome your blockers**<br><br>Deeply reflect on your answers and make any further adjustments to ensure you have a clear, concrete and prioritized **commitment** for your future **leadership development and growth**<br><br>List the proposed key commitments and actions you will take to turn your development objective into reality, including how you will get support and feedback from others to help meet your development objective |
| | |
| Step 13 | **Further reflection – Drivers in the broader leadership context:**<br>You could now turn to think about your **broader leadership work, activities and behaviors** beyond the specific development objective you were exploring<br><br>Think about all your answers to Steps 7 to 10 where you uncovered **potential drivers in yourself**. In what other leadership situations or contexts could you make these **a very positive contributor**? Are there any potential leadership situations where these **drivers might become negative blockers**? |

**Fig. 10.1** Continued

| Step 14 | **Further reflection – Blockers in the broader leadership context:** Think about all your answers to Steps 3 to 6 where **you uncovered potential blockers in yourself.** In what **different leadership situations or contexts** could you make these blockers become **a very positive contributor**? In effect, to turn these weaknesses into strengths? |
|---|---|
| | |

**Fig. 10.1** Continued

## 10.8 Appendix 8: Drivers and Blockers Exploration Tool—Mini Case Study Full Research Examples

### 10.8.1 Example A: Stefanie[1]—Female—Chief Operating Officer, Energy Company

Development Objective Explored: Ineffective Leadership Communication and Engagement

| | Tool question | Stefanie's responses in going through the drivers and blockers surfacing methodology |
|---|---|---|
| **First phase** Step 1 | **Leadership aspiration and specific development objective** Briefly state your overall **leadership aspiration** (or vision) for yourself as a leader into the future to be the "best leader you could be" | My vision is to lead a quality-based, efficient, effective and growing organization, where I motivate and inspire our people to embark on the changes needed and ensure execution with commitment. I want to role model openness and trust with high-level technical excellence. |

*(continued)*

---

[1] An example from our research (see Sect. 10.1, Example 38).

|  | Tool question | Stefanie's responses in going through the drivers and blockers surfacing methodology |
|---|---|---|
| Step 2 | State **one** specific **development objective** for change in yourself. Also state your **rationale** for making this change in your leadership behaviors. Then, briefly explain how succeeding in this objective will help you achieve your leadership aspiration. Be explicit and focused in stating this development objective or goal rather than being too general (e.g. "deep active listening" rather than "more emotionally intelligent" or "becoming a better leader") | My development objective: I want to be a more inspiring and motivating communicator with impact over a wider range of employees and stakeholders in my organization.<br>I received feedback from my CEO, board and team (including my division wide engagement survey results) that perceives me to be a leader who fails to inspire enthusiasm, seems to lack confidence in what I believe (or say) is important, and appears dismissive and aloof with others. This also includes impressions of me as a "change demander" who is sometimes dictatorial.<br>My leadership aspiration requires effective and engaging communication to support business change initiatives, and to give a sense of purpose and urgency to the initiatives I lead to achieve more concrete results—and have people committed to the outcomes. My communication style and approach will affect the way people see me as their leader. |

|  | Tool question | Stefanie's responses in going through the drivers and blockers surfacing methodology |
|---|---|---|
| Second phase | **Exploring your blockers** | |
| Step 3 | List down the **current specific behaviors** that you are doing that are preventing you from achieving your personal leadership development objective stated in Step 2. This list might include behaviors or actions that you are not doing, that are contributing to your problem or issue<br>Next, for each current specific item in your list, put the **completely opposite behavior** for this in brackets next to each item | I avoid public presentations on issues in the business as much as possible. (would do a large number of regular public presentations)<br>I rely almost entirely on communicating in set meeting situations with a small group of people who work for me by directly outlining the actions that need to be taken with limited discussion time. (would meet very regularly, formally and informally with unconstrained discussion time)<br>I use e-mail and documents to communicate most of the time with my peers in other divisions, and with people not directly reporting to me. (would make all communication personal and interpersonal)<br>If I have to speak to the whole team, I prepare detailed notes and read these aloud. (would make communication always impromptu)<br>I tend not to listen to people unless they first send me a memo on what they want to talk about. (would never request advance information)<br>I do not use emotion or visuals in my communication. (would always use emotion and visuals in every piece of communication) |
| Step 4 | Look at the list of **completely opposite behaviors** you described in Step 3. Imagine that you are now behaving in this completely opposite way<br>Do you have any **concerns, fears, worries, anxieties** or any other **negative emotions, feelings or thoughts,** if you imagine yourself behaving in these completely opposite ways? If so, what are these concerns and fears? | If I have a more energetic and engaging communication style, I fear that I will not have things to say that seem substantial and intellectual, that I may seem unprepared, or appear soft and fuzzy; and therefore, appear less competent and less in control.<br>I am also concerned that I would appear inauthentic.<br>Without preparation communication makes me feel very uncomfortable—as I expect others to be prepared. |

*(continued)*

| | Tool question | Stefanie's responses in going through the drivers and blockers surfacing methodology |
|---|---|---|
| Step 5 | What **reasons** do you have, or **what assumptions** are you making for yourself, that could explain your negative concerns, feelings or fears identified in Step 4? | Intellectual prowess is the measure of competence<br>"Talkers" are not "doers".<br>Style and energy are not really important compared to the substance.<br>I don't think I am really suited to a lot of expression, and it makes me uncomfortable. |
| Step 6 | Carefully consider your answers to Step 5. Think about your **personal characteristics (such as personality, values, beliefs, attitudes, motivations); as well as your professional and personal life experiences.** Which of these characteristics and/or experiences would explain or underpin your **reasons and assumptions** answered in Step 5? (do not be concerned that there may be duplication of answers here compared to those above) | Values of rationality and stability.<br>Highly analytical business executive.<br>Strong introvert. |
| Third phase | **Exploring your drivers** | |
| Step 7 | Imagine you absolutely achieved your development objective stated in Step 2. Describe the **new or changed behaviors** you would be exhibiting. (these would be similar to those opposite behaviors you described to yourself in Step 3—but are now a much **more realistic list of behaviors**, rather than completely opposite behaviors) | I will be an engaging, animated communicator who people want to listen to—and am a visible presence to my division people.<br>I will listen actively, stay connected and give others time to express their views.<br>I will include visual and emotional elements in my public communication in addition to facts—I am competent and interactive.<br>I will explain and listen for as much "why" as "what" and "how".<br>I will spend more face-to-face time with a wider range of my colleagues. |
| Step 8 | Reflect upon the new or changed behaviors you described in Step 7. What are the **positive emotions, feelings or thoughts** you are likely to have, or the **benefits** you might derive or see, if you achieve this change or behave in these new ways | I would feel highly professional and energized.<br>I would feel more like a leader delivering tangible results that people want to pursue.<br>I would portray the image of a strong leader. |

|  | Tool question | Stefanie's responses in going through the drivers and blockers surfacing methodology |
|---|---|---|
| Step 9 | What **reasons** do you have, or what **assumptions** are you making that could explain your positive feelings or the potential benefits identified in Step 8? | More people will respect me, and I will have a wider influence in the organization. I will be less frustrated with the pace and effectiveness of the business initiatives we are pursuing, seeing the chance to accelerate results. I will be more connected to my people; and they are likely to better understand what and why we are pursuing priorities. |
| Step 10 | Carefully consider your answers to Step 9. Think about your **personal characteristics (such as personality, values, beliefs, attitudes, motivations); as well as your professional and personal life experiences.** Also think about your own **strengths and talents.** Which of these characteristics and/or experiences and/or strengths would explain or underpin your **reasons and assumptions** answered in Step 9? (do not be concerned that there may be duplication of answers here compared to those above) | Values of results orientation, teamwork and authority. My introversion should make me a better listener. I have strong ethics. |
| Fourth phase | **Insights, commitments and actions** | |
| Step 11 | Reflection and insights: What deep **insights emerged for you** about your assumptions, influences, **drivers and blockers** across your answers in Steps 3–10? Summarize your insights here. How do these insights compare and contrast with any feedback you may have received? | Substance and engagement are not mutually exclusive I can be a more active communicator and listener whilst demonstrating competence—I need to find my right balance. If I am perceived as more engaging, and people commit to the business initiatives, more concrete and timely results will be achieved. |

*(continued)*

|  | Tool question | Stefanie's responses in going through the drivers and blockers surfacing methodology |
|---|---|---|
| Step 12 | Restated aspiration, development objective and commitments: Take some time now to **reflect** on these **insights** and consider the **implications** for your own leadership development, as well as the actions you will need to take to achieve your development objective<br>Re-state your leadership aspiration and your development objective to include these insights, and propose your concrete actions for change (including experimentation) that **unleash your drivers and overcome your blockers**<br>Deeply reflect on your answers and make any further adjustments to ensure you have a clear, concrete and prioritized **commitment** for your future **leadership development and growth**<br>List the proposed key commitments and actions you will take to turn your development objective into reality, including how you will get support and feedback from others to help meet your development objective | Implications: I will need to set more time aside for communication activities and change the way I plan and deliver these. Restated development objective with actions:<br>**I will be an** inspiring, motivating and engaging communicator with leadership impact over a wider range of employees in my organization, so there is mutual commitment and a shared sense of purpose. **Therefore, I commit to**:<br>Increasing my time and effort in being a visible presence to my division people and providing direct time in my schedule for this;<br>Listening actively, staying connected and giving others time to express their views in meetings and discussions.<br>Including visual and emotional elements in my public communication in addition to facts and getting training in this;<br>Preparing my communication to explain as much "why" as "what" including asking more questions of others; and<br>Spending more face-to-face time with a wider range of my colleagues.<br>I have updated the development objective in language that makes sense to me. This matter is also included as the first item in my quarterly reviews with the CEO for feedback.<br>I will take on communication coaching support—and seek feedback from my peers.<br>I will review and amend my forward diary and meeting plans to organize time with peers, and give more discussion including moving other team member items ahead of my own in agendas.<br>I commit to being a more effective communicator and leader. |

|  | Tool question | Stefanie's responses in going through the drivers and blockers surfacing methodology |
| --- | --- | --- |
| Step 13 | Broader leadership context: You could now turn to think about your **broader leadership work, activities and behaviors** beyond the specific development objective you were exploring Think about all your answers to Steps 7–10 where you uncovered **potential drivers in yourself.** In what other leadership situations or contexts could you make these **a very positive contributor?** Are there any potential leadership situations where these **drivers might become negative blockers?** | My value of teamwork should be a positive driver in working with project teams—including those with members outside my division. My values of results orientation and authority should be a positive driver if I need to lead and manage in a crisis situation. However, these values could also become blockers if the situation means developing capabilities in a person I lead, yet I end up micro-managing them. |
| Step 14 | Another reflection: Think about all your answers to Steps 3–6 where **you uncovered potential blockers in yourself.** In what **different leadership situations or contexts** could you make these blockers become **a very positive contributor?** In effect, to turn these weaknesses into strengths? | My capacity for analytics could be better used as a "thought partner" to give others advice and contribute to their ideas not just critique them—becoming more of a 'trusted adviser'. My behavior of detailed written communication could be better targeted to act as a thorough follow up to assist people with further information and implementation rather than acting as a 'screen out' at the beginning. My value of stability could be more on display in empathizing with people as they face change in our organization. Sharing this in dialogue would connect with people rather than acting as a frustration—for them and myself. |

## 10.8.2 Example B: Markus[2]—Male—Chief Executive Officer, Regional Consumer Retail Company

Development Objective Explored: Domineering Control, and Micro-management

| | Tool question | Markus responses in going through the drivers and blockers surfacing methodology |
|---|---|---|
| First phase | **Leadership aspiration and specific development objective** | |
| Step 1 | Briefly state your overall **leadership aspiration** (or vision) for yourself as a leader into the future to be the "best leader you could be" | I aspire to lead the region's best retail company, renowned for its quality of products and services and the value it creates for its customers, employees and shareholders; and to grow this business into a global enterprise. As its leader, I want to be seen as visionary and dynamic, as well as trusted and respected. |
| Step 2 | State **one** specific **development objective** for change in yourself. Also state your **rationale** for making this change in your leadership behaviors. Then, briefly explain how succeeding in this objective will help you achieve your leadership aspiration. Be explicit and focused in stating this development objective or goal rather than being too general (e.g. "deep active listening" rather than "more emotionally intelligent" or "becoming a better leader") | My development objective: I want to reduce my micro-managing and direct involvement with day-to-day operations and interference with my direct reports.<br>This would help shift my time and effort to strategic growth initiatives for the company, and reduce personal stress.<br>Feedback from my chairperson and some directors shows impatience with progress on the business growth initiatives, notwithstanding very good operational results. They are also concerned about the turnover of senior leaders in the business, and the absence of a COO role.<br>A recent 360-degree survey showed my executive team regards me as a micro-manager with too much time spent in ongoing operations. They perceive me as decisive, action oriented and directive, yet closed-minded and not giving each of the divisional leaders the authority and empowerment to fully carry out their roles. Three senior executives have left the company in the past two years for roles they say give them more scope for leading, even though these are with smaller organizations.<br>I have strongly resisted appointing a COO because I want to remain close to the operating divisions.<br>Achieving my leadership aspiration requires the ability to grow the business by giving time and effort to strategic initiatives and having a talented and stable team to implement this into the future. |

[2] An example from our research (see Sect. 10.1, Example 39).

|  | Tool question | Markus responses in going through the drivers and blockers surfacing methodology |
|---|---|---|
| **Second phase** | **Exploring your blockers** | |
| Step 3 | List down the **current specific behaviors** that you are doing that are preventing you from achieving your personal leadership development objective stated in Step 2. This list might include behaviors or actions that you are not doing, that are contributing to your problem or issue. Next, for each current specific item in your list, put the **completely opposite behavior** for this in brackets next to each item | Directly intervening with the subordinates of my direct reports. (Never intervening) Insisting on my giving the final approval for business unit decisions such as managerial appointments and participating in the recruitment interviews for these. (delegate all approvals) Chairing business plan meetings of each business unit and division. (Never chairing these meetings) Directly managing the five operating divisions, with their leaders reporting straight to me (e.g. I also make field visits without the need to involve the division head). (Complete delegation and empowerment) Avoid having a COO. (Appoint a COO and empower them) Re-writing most board submissions from my direct reports. (Never re-write these reports) Spending most of my time on current operations rather than on future plans or developing future leaders. (Devote all my time to strategic and people development) |
| Step 4 | Look at the list of **completely opposite behaviors** you described in Step 3. Imagine that you are now behaving in this completely opposite way Do you have any **concerns, fears, worries, anxieties** or any other **negative emotions, feelings or thoughts,** if you imagine yourself behaving in these completely opposite ways? If so, what are these concerns and fears? | If I were to do the opposite of these, I am fearful that results will not be achieved to the level we achieve now. I am anxious that the people I would empower or delegate to will not drive the business with the same sense of energy and urgency I have. By distancing myself from daily operations I will not have the control visibility I like, and there will be more "surprises". I am uncomfortable with the idea of a COO having the knowledge and power that comes from direct control; and becoming a competitor to me. The strategic growth initiatives will take time and energy to work through and may not yield results in the short term. |
| Step 5 | What **reasons** do you have, or what **assumptions** are you making for yourself, that could explain your negative concerns, feelings or fears identified in Step 4? | Direct control leads to better results and better manages risks. The CEO should understand every aspect of their business and be very visible. I am recognized and rewarded based on results. I find it difficult to really trust other people to do the job as well as I can. Changing this means a lot of effort in their development. I made it the hard way—why create a CEO platform for someone else. Making these changes will mean I'm more reliant on other people, and things might take more time. |

*(continued)*

|  | Tool question | Markus responses in going through the drivers and blockers surfacing methodology |
|---|---|---|
| Step 6 | Carefully consider your answers to Step 5. Think about your **personal characteristics** (such as personality, values, beliefs, attitudes, motivations); as well as your **professional and personal life experiences**. Which of these characteristics and/or experiences would explain or underpin your **reasons and assumptions** answered in Step 5? (do not be concerned that there may be duplication of answers here compared to those above) | Personal characteristics: although I display confidence, I am insecure about myself, I am quite risk-averse; and it has taken a long time to get to the top of an organization. Values—results-drive; authority; control. Talented people are valuable, but I want to minimize personal competition. Results-oriented executive in the sector, with strong market visibility. *Note: There were a number of personal/private life issues that emerged in this person's reflection including their relationship with one parent, and a painful childhood school memory that surfaced. Details for these are not included in the list above.* |
| Third phase | **Exploring your drivers** | |
| Step 7 | Imagine you absolutely achieved your development objective stated in Step 2. Describe the **new or changed behaviors** you would be exhibiting. (these would be similar to those opposite behaviors you described to yourself in Step 3—but are now a much **more realistic list of behaviors**, rather than completely opposite behaviors) | Appointing and empowering a COO. Increasing delegated authorities to the senior business unit leaders. Stopping direct interventions that undermine team members. Increasing the range of consultation, consensus and empowered decisions compared to directions that I am involved with. Stop re-writing board submissions from my direct reports. Acting as a "facilitator" for operational reviews; spending more time up front agreeing goals and objectives for the divisions rather than imposing these along the way. Acting more as a coach and mentor, providing more constructive feedback and demonstrating recognition/ appreciation of others. Making sure talented people can thrive. Providing the right kind of development support to improve their capacities. Re-arranging my work priorities and activities to spend substantial time on growth initiatives; and to building a more stable and committed team. |
| Step 8 | Reflect upon the new or changed behaviors you described in Step 7. What are the **positive emotions, feelings or thoughts** you are likely to have, or the **benefits** you might derive or see, if you achieve this change or behave in these new ways | I should have the time and "bandwidth" to invest in both the business and people growth for the company. Adding more exciting activities with longer term "pay offs". Reduced frustration with the daily "fires", and large reduction of time/effort in routine matters. Being perceived as a more visionary leader, not just an operating one. A higher level of overall motivation present in our business. Lower management turnover. |

|  | Tool question | Markus responses in going through the drivers and blockers surfacing methodology |
|---|---|---|
| Step 9 | What **reasons** do you have, or what **assumptions** are you making that could explain your positive feelings or the potential benefits identified in Step 8? | Increased personal and family time as a result of removing a lot of time-consuming activities.<br>Aligned recognition with the Board's objectives increases my security as CEO, and well positions me for future board roles.<br>If successful, can be perceived as a global leader in the sector.<br>Sharing more of the burden with people I enjoy working with and respect should reduce my personal stress and increase my self-confidence.<br>Organization can be seen as employer of choice, and I can leave a legacy of sustainable leadership in the business. |
| Step 10 | Carefully consider your answers to Step 9. Think about your **personal characteristics (such as personality, values, beliefs, attitudes, motivations); as well as your professional and personal life experiences.** Also think about your own **strengths and talents.** Which of these characteristics and/or experiences and/or strengths would explain or underpin your **reasons and assumptions** answered in Step 9? (do not be concerned that there may be duplication of answers here compared to those above) | Values—security; recognition; family.<br>Personal characteristics: I stress about my work-life balance; and am concerned we have a good future. These changes could solve/alleviate this.<br>This will build my business reputation and standing long run.<br>My personality requires constant challenges to stimulate and motivate me—and these changes would give me more excitement; and motivate others. |
| Fourth phase | **Insights, commitments and actions** | |
| Step 11 | Reflection and insights: What deep **insights emerged for you** about your assumptions, influences, **drivers and blockers** across your answers in Steps 3–10? Summarize your insights here. How do these insights compare and contrast with any feedback you may have received? | Spending time and effort on building my team's capacities will make the longer-term achievements more likely.<br>I should be seen more for my qualities of leadership, not just results.<br>The short term thinking I have had is making a lot of poor life trade-offs.<br>If I trust and develop people, I can feel more secure and do more interesting things.<br>A change in leadership style like this would directly respond to the feedback I've had in a very positive way.<br>A COO could be the legacy CEO I create and develop. |

*(continued)*

|  | Tool question | Markus responses in going through the drivers and blockers surfacing methodology |
|---|---|---|
| Step 12 | Restated aspiration, development objective and commitments:<br>Take some time now to **reflect** on these **insights** and consider the **implications** for your own leadership development, as well as the actions you will need to take to achieve your development objective<br>Re-state your leadership aspiration and your development objective to include these insights, and propose your concrete actions for change (including experimentation) that **unleash your drivers and overcome your blockers**<br>Deeply reflect on your answers and make any further adjustments to ensure you have a clear, concrete and prioritized **commitment** for your future **leadership development and growth**<br>List the proposed key commitments and actions you will take to turn your development objective into reality, including how you will get support and feedback from others to help meet your development objective | Implications: I will need a staged plan of behavior changes, and a complete realignment of my timetable and diary, together with some organizational changes and support.<br>Restated development objective with aspiration and actions:<br>**I will be a visionary leader with the most highly regarded leadership team in the sector.** So, my development objective is to develop my team members, delegate authority, empower leadership with them; and shift my time, effort and focus to strategic growth initiatives and talent-building for the company, as well as reduce my personal stress, and increase my sense of security.<br>**So, I am committing to these changes:**<br>Create a change plan for myself to implement over the next six months.<br>Appoint a COO and having others in my team and the board help make that selection; as well as changing the formal authorities and delegations.<br>Re-arrange my weekly timetable to spend substantial time on new business growth initiatives; and empowering leaders for these activities as they move into the operationalization phase.<br>Stop the direct interventions that undermine my team members. Where field visits occur, these will be led and managed by the responsible leader.<br>Stop re-writing board submissions from my direct reports. Encourage peer review of important board papers, but give the authority for submission to the executive, except for the strategic initiative papers. COO to act as the co-sign off with the executive on operational reports.<br>Increase the range of consultation, consensus and empowered decisions compared to directions that I have been involved with.<br>Act as a "facilitator" for yearly operational reviews; and encouraging the new COO to spend more time up front agreeing goals and objectives for the divisions rather than imposing these along the way as I have been doing.<br>Seek the team's input and involvement with an ongoing series of "vision" sessions throughout the organization.<br>Increase at home (non-work time) by six hours a week, and making one weekend day completely work free. Get my family to give me feedback.<br>Having an annual feedback survey focused on the changes to leadership approach I am committing to; getting a new mentor/coach with experience in this kind of personal change. I will need some easy to use stress management techniques, so if I feel I want to intervene again, I can hold myself back. I will also need some additional skills in giving/receiving effective feedback. |

|  | Tool question | Markus responses in going through the drivers and blockers surfacing methodology |
|---|---|---|
| Step 13 | Broader leadership context: You could now turn to think about your **broader leadership work, activities and behaviors** beyond the specific development objective you were exploring. Think about all your answers to Steps 7–10 where you uncovered **potential drivers in yourself**. In what other leadership situations or contexts could you make these **a very positive contributor?** Are there any potential leadership situations where these **drivers might become negative blockers?** | The values and motivators of family and security should drive me to make my changes. My personality desires for curiosity, constant challenges, and stimulation, should make me more "strategic" when oversighting the business as CEO. Nevertheless, this could become a negative to block my leadership changes, if people perceive my questioning here as reverting to micro interference; if I don't work closely with the COO to ensure we are working as a partnership; and if I don't empower the leaders of the new businesses. I need to watch that my risk aversion does not inappropriately constrain the "empowered" ideas of the leadership team. |
| Step 14 | Another reflection: Think about all your answers to Steps 3–6 where **you uncovered potential blockers in yourself.** In what **different leadership situations or contexts** could you make these blockers become **a very positive contributor?** In effect, to turn these weaknesses into strengths? | The level and range of my experience could be used to help accelerate the development of others. I could do some more coaching/lecturing as part of our company's training academy. The negative experiences of my own leadership journey could be used as examples for others not to follow, if I am successful in making the changes I want. *Note: Following three months of coaching and implementation of his plan, Markus added the following to his analysis, based on reflection. "I have clearly not paid enough attention to self-awareness in the past. I should disclose my negative experiences and their consequences to others, no matter whether I succeed in the change or not. This would actually demonstrate self-awareness without using the control I have craved in the past—and show the dangers of being a 'control freak'." He also appointed a COO and instituted the organizational changes he intended.* |

### 10.8.3 Example C: John[3]—Male—Chief Operating Officer, Transport Company

Development Objective Explored: Lack of Assertiveness

| | Tool question | John's responses in going through the drivers and blockers surfacing methodology |
|---|---|---|
| **First phase** | **Leadership aspiration and development objective** | |
| Step 1 | Briefly state your overall **leadership aspiration** (or vision) for yourself as a leader into the future | My vision is to prove myself as a viable and effective general executive of large organizations.<br>My aspiration is to improve my ability to lead teams of senior executives with higher knowledge and experience than myself in their areas of expertise.<br>When it comes time for me to lead a large organization or an entire company, I want to be completely confident that I am fit for the leadership role, even if I do not have direct, in-depth knowledge of all the functional areas of the organization. |
| Step 2 | State one **specific development objective** for change you have identified as important; and state your rationale for making this change in your leadership behaviors. Also briefly explain how succeeding in this objective will help you achieve your leadership aspiration | I want to be more assertive in my professional environment and, specifically, with the managerial team for which I am responsible. |
| **Second phase** | **Exploring blockers** | |
| Step 3 | State the **current specific behaviors** that are preventing you from achieving your personal leadership development objective stated in Step 2 | I put excessive emphasis on reaching consensus within the team and I delay decisions that could generate divisions and conflicts.<br>I refrain from criticizing people openly.<br>I employ a formal style of communication.<br>I do not take a clear stand when there are different opinions in the room. |
| Step 4 | Imagine that you are behaving in **the completely opposite way** to the behaviors you described in Step 3<br>Do you have any concerns, fears, worries or any other **negative emotions, feelings or thoughts,** if you imagine yourself behaving in these completely opposite ways? If so, what are these concerns? | The team could break apart as a consequence of decisions I take without the agreement of all team-members.<br>I would lose the support of some members of the team and, ultimately, I would become a leader with no followers. |

---

[3] An example from our research (see Sect. 10.1, Example 41).

|  | Tool question | John's responses in going through the drivers and blockers surfacing methodology |
|---|---|---|
| Step 5 | What **reasons** do you have, or **what assumptions** are you making, that could **explain** your negative concerns, feelings or fears identified in Step 4? | Assertiveness destroys interpersonal relationships. |
| Step 6 | Carefully consider your answers to Step 5. What important **values, beliefs, attitudes, motivations or personal characteristics (such as personality)** do you have, that would explain or underpin your **reasons and assumptions** answered in Step 5? | Harmony and friendship are core values that are deeply rooted in my personality. Decisions taken "against" somebody's will could threaten the harmony of the team and prove disrespectful to my friends and team members. At the same time, I do not put much value in a respectful explanation of different views that would eventually lead to a decision in which one of the parties is unhappy with the outcome. As an aspect of my personality, I believe that expressing oneself can hardly compensate for the frustration that arises from losing an argument or not winning the favor of the superior decision-maker. |
| Third phase | Exploring drivers | |
| Step 7 | Imagine you absolutely achieved your development objective stated in Step 2. Describe the **new or changed behaviors** you would be exhibiting. (these would be similar to those you imagined for yourself in Step 4) | I am decisive in all circumstances. I give both positive and constructive feedback to all members of the team, regardless of their seniority or their technical expertise. I practice tough empathy (tough on issues, soft on people). My communication style is less formal when I am in a larger circle of colleagues. |
| Step 8 | Reflect on the new or changed behaviors you described in Step 7. What are the **positive emotions, feelings or thoughts** you are likely to have, or the **benefits** you might derive, feel or see, if you **achieve this change**? | I feel proud and satisfied to drive things forward and achieve results more quickly. I feel more confident of being a viable leader of large organizations, where a wide range of different technical skills is required. Change has become more easily achievable and less extraordinary within the team. |
| Step 9 | What **reasons** do you have, or what **assumptions** are you making that could explain your positive feelings or the potential benefits identified in Step 8? | Team members will respect me more as an assertive leader. The frustration within the team that arises from excessively long discussions and delayed decisions will decrease. My communication skills will improve as I make it a habit to clearly explain the reasons for my decisions. |

*(continued)*

|  | Tool question | John's responses in going through the drivers and blockers surfacing methodology |
|---|---|---|
| Step 10 | Carefully consider your answers to Step 9. What important **values, beliefs, attitudes, motivations or personal characteristics (such as personality)** do you have, that would explain or underpin your **reasons and assumptions** answered in Step 9? | The credibility of a leader increases when his/her team achieves its objective with appropriate effort and within a reasonable amount of time.<br>Team-members show respect for their leader when their efforts are not wasted, and their commitment is correctly taken into consideration.<br>People understand—or at least show respect and feel considered—only if decisions are clearly justified and explained. |
| Fourth phase | **Insights, commitments and actions** | |
| Step 11 | Reflection and insights: What deep **insights emerged for you** about your assumptions, influences, **drivers and blockers** across your answers to Steps 3–10? Summarize your insights. How do these insights compare and contrast with any feedback you have received? | Contrary to aggressiveness, assertiveness does not destroy interpersonal relationships. A leader must take a clear stance when the team has different views on a specific issue. If he does not and a decision is not taken after reasonable time or effort, the team-members cease to believe in the effectiveness of the leadership and stop being followers.<br>Communication is a key aspect of assertiveness and it can overcome the short-term disengagement that supporters of "losing views" could feel after a decision is taken. |

|  | Tool question | John's responses in going through the drivers and blockers surfacing methodology |
|---|---|---|
| Step 12 | Take some time to further **reflect** on these **insights** and consider the **implications** for your own leadership development, as well as the actions you will need to take to achieve your desired development objective Re-state your development objective to include these insights, and propose your concrete actions for change (including experimentation, practice, support and feedback) that will **unleash your drivers and overcome your blockers** Deeply reflect on your answer now; and make any further adjustments to ensure you have a clear, concrete and prioritized **commitment** for your future **leadership development and growth**. Ensure you list the key actions you will take to turn your development objective into reality, including how you will get support and feedback from others to meet your objective | Implications: I need to create a clear framework for discussions and decision-making within the team where everybody has an opportunity to present and motivate his/her views, but also where effective and transparent decisions are taken at the end of the process. The framework implies a set of organized meetings/tools for the whole team and new one-to-one communication channels between myself and my team-members Restated development objective with actions: **I will be an** assertive leader capable of listening to the different positions in the management team and in the respective parts of the organization I am responsible for. After reasonable time and effort are spent to review such positions, I will take appropriate decisions and justify them to the team in an open and transparent manner. So, I commit to: Ensuring opportunities for everybody in the team to express their motivated views and concerns; Taking decisions in all circumstances, even when different positions are evident; Refraining from delaying decisions only because I hope a unanimous position will be achieved in the future; Making sure the drivers behind any decision/position I express are clearly communicated across the organization. I will hold regular staff meetings where a framework for discussion and decision-making is established and known to each staff member. I will encourage my staff members to speak openly about their concerns and reasons for not supporting others' views within the team. I will seek regular feedback from my team-members in regular one-to-one meetings about the effectiveness of the decision-making process and my communication. I will create "communication events" in my schedule to engage the team and the organization in Q&A sessions on the status of the company, objectives, future agenda, challenges and workplan. |

*(continued)*

|  | Tool question | John's responses in going through the drivers and blockers surfacing methodology |
|---|---|---|
| Step 13 | You now turn to think about your **broader leadership work, activities and behaviors** beyond the specific development objective you were exploring. Reflect on all your answers to Steps 7–10 where you uncovered **potential drivers in yourself**. In what other leadership situations or contexts can you make these **a very positive contributor**? Are there any potential leadership situations where these **drivers might become negative blockers?** | Increased assertiveness leads to more and better decisions and accelerates the pace at which the team achieves its objectives. A team led assertively produces more results. On the other hand, voicing one's assertiveness on all occasions, including those situations where "political caution" must be exercised, can cause misunderstandings in relation to the managerial style in place. It is not always simple to master successfully the limit between assertive and aggressive leadership. |
| Step 14 | Reflect upon, and think about all your answers to Steps 3–6 where **you uncovered potential blockers in yourself.** In what **different leadership situations or contexts** could you make these blockers become **a very positive contributor**? In effect, to turn the **weakness into a strength?** | When the complexity of the organization and the area of responsibility grow, the mix of skills required in leading the teams also changes. In a larger context, a formal communication style and a more cautious approach to decisions with far-reaching impact can also be an advantage. Different country and corporate cultures could require more or less visible degrees of assertiveness. When one is active as a representative of the industry or at a corporate level, beyond the boundary of one's company or division, consensus is the only available option for achieving a decision. In this context, being consensus-oriented becomes an advantage. The same applies to relationships with government agencies or public authorities. |

Note for readers—this is an earlier example where the questions in the steps were slightly different than the final version of the tool. It is presented accurately at the time of doing that field research

## 10.9 Appendix 9: Potential Relationship of Exploring Drivers and Blockers with a Selection of Leadership and Development Theories, Models, Frames and Approaches

The exploration of Drivers and Blockers can lead to enhanced self-awareness, so its application and utility can be complementary to a wide range of leadership development approaches, including:

| Theory, model, approach | Description |
| --- | --- |
| Self-awareness | Self-awareness is "the extent to which [individuals'] self-perceptions are internally integrated and congruent with the way others perceive them" (Hall, 2004, p. 154) |
| Adaptive leadership | Adaptive leadership is the, "practice of mobilizing people to tackle tough challenges and thrive" (Heifetz et al., 2009) |
| Authentic leadership | Authentic leadership is "a process that draws from both positive psychological capacities and a highly developed organizational context, which results in both greater self-awareness and self-regulated positive behaviors on the part of leaders and associates, fostering positive self-development" (Luthans & Avolio, 2003, p. 243) |
| Emotional intelligence | Emotional Intelligence is "the ability to perceive emotions, to access and generate emotions so as to assist thought, to understand emotions and emotional knowledge, and to reflectively regulate emotions so as to produce emotional and intellectual growth" (Mayer & Salovey, 1997, p. 5) |
| Identity | Identity refers to the, "vast domain of meanings attached to the self and comprising the content and organization of self-concepts" (Gecas, 1982, p. 10). Self-concept is comprised of many identities that differ along aspects such as their significance to the individual, whether they represent real or prospective accomplishment, and temporal perspective, ranging through past, present or future (Ibarra & Petriglieri, 2010) |
| Personalization | Personalization is a process, "by which individuals examine their experiences and revisit their life stories as part and parcel of management learning" (Petriglieri, Wood, & Petriglieri, 2011, p. 436). Personalization promotes learning by "integrating past, present and future; cognitive and emotional; personal and professional aspects of the individual's life" (Petriglieri et al., 2011, p. 445) |
| Transformational and charismatic leadership | Charismatic leadership theory (Bass, 1985), an extension of attribution theory, states that charismatic leaders have a cogent and persuasive vision, are persistent and know what they are aiming for and how to get there. It is this vision and the way it is communicated which inspires people to dedicate themselves to organizational progress (Bromley & Kirschner- Bromley, 2007) The transformational leadership theory states that transformational leaders are deeply trusted, respected and acknowledged by their followers. Transformational leaders inspire their followers to place more stress on organizational goals rather than their personal ones and commit to the shared vision (Bass & Avolio, 1993). Transformational leaders have the quality of being influential, persuasive and charismatic, while stimulating employee development by empowering employees and aligning their personal objectives with the organizational objectives (Bass & Avolio, 1993) |

*(continued)*

| Theory, model, approach | Description |
| --- | --- |
| Transactional and Leader–member exchange (LMX) theory | According to Transactional leadership theory (Burns, 1978), leadership is a mutual relationship or a "quid pro quo" between leaders and their followers where leaders inspire their employees to attain the specific task by elucidating requirements and essentials of that task and then acknowledging and rewarding them for their work. If the employees fail to complete the assigned task, they may get punished (Bromley & Kirschner-Bromley, 2007)<br>LMX theory outlines aspects of leader- follower association where high-quality associations are centered on trust and mutual respect, whereas low quality associations are developed on fulfillment of contracts. This approach assumes that leaders behave differently to different employees as a result of which some employees feel ignored (Graen & Uhl-Bien, 1995). Those who feel included consider their leaders as transformational whereas those ignored consider their leaders to have a transactional approach (Graen & Uhl-Bien, 1995) |
| Values-based leadership | Values-Based Leadership (VBL) outlines the association between a leader and followers predicated on a mutual commitment to ideological values articulated by a leader (House & Aditya, 1997) |
| Intentional change theory | According to "Intentional Change Theory", the change process comprises a series of "discoveries", which work as a continuous cycle in bringing about sustainable and long lasting change in individuals (Boyatzis, 2006) |
| Positive leadership and psychology | The field of positive psychology follows that, "what is good about life is as genuine as what is bad and therefore deserves equal attention" (Peterson & Seligman, 2004, p. 4). The movement is led by Seligman (1998a, 1998b) and other psychologists, for example, Ed Diener (2000), Christopher Peterson (2000) and Rick Snyder (2000), who argue for a need to focus on strengths and adaptability in people, rather than continuing on the path of looking into and fixing negatives or weaknesses |
| Adult mind development | Kegan (1994) adult development theory examines the ways humans develop and change over their lives. Kegan (1994) presents a developmental model that provides the trajectory of mental complexity, dividing the latter into five levels: impulsive mind, instrumental mind, the socialized mind, self-authoring mind, and self-transforming mind with the self-transforming mind being the highest level one could reach. Each level involves, "looking at" a paradigm, which during the previous level, one could only manage to "look through" (Kegan, 1994) |

| Theory, model, approach | Description |
| --- | --- |
| Immunity to change and competing commitments | The notion of 'competing commitments' offers an important perspective that looks into change and conceives human behavior (Kegan & Lahey, 2001a, 2009). Competing commitments serve as the hidden "assumptions" of individuals or groups. They have been described as the reasons, often beyond the conscious level (constituents of unconscious), responsible for the failure of accomplishing change, that an individual was initially committed to (McAvoy & Butler, 2005) |
| Mindfulness | Mindfulness relates to the "quality of consciousness that is characterized by clarity and vividness of current experience and functioning and thus stands in contrast to the mindless, less "awake" states of habitual or automatic functioning that may be chronic for many individuals" (Kirk & Ryan, 2003). Mindfulness has been shown to mitigate negative functioning and promote positive results in various significant areas of life (Brown, Ryan, & Creswell, 2007; Hafenbrack, 2014; Kudesia, 2017; Langer, 2009; Shaffakat, et al. 2017) |
| Traditional leadership theories, trait, behavioral and so forth | According to the trait approach, leaders possess certain traits that differentiate them from others. Intelligence and dominance were the two traits that were found to be related to leadership (Mann, 1959; Stogdill, 1948). It further suggests that these traits are integral to the individual's DNA and connotes that organizations should concentrate on selection rather than development of leaders (Grint, 2005). Behavioral approach concentrates on the behaviors demonstrated by the leaders, the way they act and work with their followers. Research by University of Michigan (Katz, Maccoby, Gurin, & Floor, 1951) and Ohio State University (Stogdill & Coons, 1957) recognized two aspects of leadership centered on employees and production |

# References

Allen, S. J., & Hartman, N. S. (2008). Sources of learning: An exploratory study. *Organization Development Journal, 26*(2), 75–87.

Altorfer, O. (1992). How can we help one worker? *Journal for Quality and Participation, 15*(4), 88–93.

Anderson, C. R. (1977). Locus of control, coping behaviors, and performance in a stress setting: A longitudinal study. *Journal of Applied Psychology, 62*(4), 446–451.

Andrews, G., Singh, M., & Bond, M. (1993). The defense style questionnaire. *The Journal of Nervous and Mental Disease, 18*(4), 246–256.

Antonacopoulou, E. P., & Gabriel, Y. (2001). Emotion, learning and organizational change: Towards an integration of psychoanalytic and other perspectives. *Journal of Organizational Change Management, 14*(5), 435–451.

Ardi, D. (2013). *The Fall of the Alphas: The New Beta Way to Connect, Collaborate, Influence—and Lead*. New York: St. Martin's Press.

Ashford, S. J. (1988). Individual strategies for coping with stress during organizational transitions. *Journal of Applied Behavioral Science, 24*(1), 19–36.

Ashforth, B. E., & Lee, R. T. (1990). Defensive behavior in organizations: A preliminary model. *Human Relations, 43*(7), 621–648.

Aspinwall, L. G., & Staudinger, U. M. (2003). *A psychology of human strengths: Fundamental questions and future directions for a positive psychology*. Washington, DC: American Psychological Association.

Atwater, L., Wang, M., Smither, J. W., & Fleenor, J. W. (2009). Are cultural characteristics associated with the relationship between self and others' ratings of leadership? *Journal of Applied Psychology, 94*(4), 876.

Avolio, B. J., Luthans, F., & Walumba, F. O. (2004). *Authentic Leadership: Theory Building for Veritable Sustained Performance* (Working Paper Series).

Bachkirova, T. (2011). *Developmental coaching: Working with the self*. Maidenhead, UK: Open University Press.

Bagozzi, R. P., Verbeke, W., & Gavino, J. C. (2003). Culture moderates the self-regulation of shame and its effects on performance: The case of salespersons in the Netherlands and the Philippines. *Journal of Applied Psychology, 88*(2), 219–233.

Bandura, A. (1997). *Self-efficacy: The exercise of control*. New York: W. H. Freeman and company.

Banerjee, R. P. (2003). Organisational character: Issues, imperatives and practices. *International Journal of Human Resources Development and Management, 3*(1), 72. https://doi.org/10.1504/IJHRDM.2003.001047

Bardi, A., Lee, J. A., Hofmann-Towfigh, N., & Soutar, G. (2009). The structure of intraindividual value change. *Journal of Personality and Social Psychology, 97*(5), 913–929. https://doi.org/10.1037/a0016617

Barrick, M. R., & Mount, M. K. (1991). The Big Five personality dimensions and job performance: A meta-analysis. *Personnel Psychology, 44*(1), 1–26.

Barrick, M. R., Mount, M. K., & Strauss, J. P. (1993). Conscientiousness and performance of sales representatives: Test for the mediating effect of goal setting. *Journal of Applied Psychology, 78*(5), 715–722.

Barringer, B. R. (2008). *The truth about starting a business*. New Jersey: Pearson Education, Inc.

Barsade, S. G., Ramarajan, L., & Westen, D. (2009). Implicit affect in organizations. *Research in Organizational Behavior, 29*, 135–162.

Bass, B. M. (1985). *Leadership and performance beyond expectations*. New York: Free Press.

Bass, B. M., & Avolio, B. J. (1993). *Manual: the multifactor leadership questionnaire*. Palo Alto, CA: Consulting Psychologist Press.

Basseches, M. (1984). *Dialectical thinking and adult development*. Norwood, NJ: Ablex.

Bates, K. L. (2006). *Study: Type A personality not linked to heart disease*. Retrieved from http://www.ur.umich.edu/0607/Sept05_06/03.shtml

Baumeister, R. F. (1993). *Self-esteem: The puzzle of low self-regard*. New York: Plenum Press.

Baumeister, R. F. (1999). *The self in social psychology*. Philadelphia, PA: Psychology Press.

Beechler, S., & Woodward, I. C. (2009). The global "war for talent." *Journal of International Management, 15*(3), 273–285.

Benjamin, S. (2014). Five crazy things Steve Ballmer has done. Retrieved May 31, 2014, from http://fortune.com/2014/05/31/steve-ballmer-crazy/

Berger, J. G., Hasegawa, B. A., Hammerman, J., & Kegan, R. (2007). How consciousness develops adequate complexity to deal with a complex world: The subject-object theory of Robert Kegan.

Berry, D. R., Bagby, R., Smerz, J., Rinaldo, J. C., Caldwell-Andrews, A., & Baer, R. A. (2001). Effectiveness of NEO-PI-R Research Validity Scales for Discriminating Analog Malingering and Genuine Psychopathology. *Journal of Personality Assessment*, 76(3), 496–516.

Billing, T. K., & Steverson, P. (2013). Moderating role of Type-A personality on stress-outcome relationships. *Management Decision*, 51(9), 1893–1904.

Bing, M. N., & Lounsbury, J. W. (2000). Openness and job performance in U.S.-based Japanese manufacturing companies. *Journal of Business and Psychology*, 14(3), 515–522.

Blackwell, L. S., Trzesniewski, K. H., & Dweck, C. S. (2007). Implicit theories of intelligence predict achievement across an adolescent transition: A longitudinal study and an intervention. *Child Development*, 78(1), 246–263.

Bochman, D. J., & Kroth, M. (2010). Immunity to transformational learning and change. *The Learning Organization*, 17(4), 328–342. https://doi.org/10.1108/09696471011043090

Bovey, W. H., & Hede, A. (2001). Resistance to organisational change: the role of defence mechanisms. *Journal of Managerial Psychology*, 16(7), 534–548. https://doi.org/10.1108/EUM0000000006166

Bowe, C. M., Lahey, L., Armstrong, E., & Kegan, R. (2003). Questioning the "big assumptions". Part I: addressing personal contradictions that impede professional development. *Medical Education*, 37(8), 715–22.

Bowman, G. D., & Stern, M. (1995). Adjustment to occupational stress: The relationship of perceived control to effectiveness of coping strategies. *Journal of Counseling Psychology*, 42(3), 294–303.

Boyatzis, R. E. (2006). An overview of intentional change from a complexity perspective. *Journal of Management Development*, 25(7), 607–623.

Boyatzis, R. E., & Akrivou, K. (2006). The ideal self as the driver of intentional change. *Journal of Management Development*, 25(7), 624–642.

Boyatzis, R. E., & McKee, A. (2006). Intentional change. *Journal of Organizational Excellence*, 25(3), 49–60.

Boyatzis, R. E., Stubbs, E. C., & Taylor, S. N. (2002). Learning cognitive and emotional intelligence competencies through graduate management education. *Academy of Management Learning and Education*, 1(2), 150–162.

Boyle, G. J. (1997). Crisis in traditional personality assessment: Implications for military testing. In *Proceedings of the 39th Annual Conference of the International Military Testing Association* (pp. 61–64). Sydney.

Boyle, G. J., & Saklofske, D. H. (2004). *Sage benchmarks in psychology: The psychology of individual differences*. London, UK: Sage Publications.

Boyle, G. J., Stankov, L., & Cattell, R. B. (1995). Measurement and statistical models in the study of personality and intelligence. In D. H. Saklofske & M. Zeidner (Eds.), *International handbook of personality and intelligence* (pp. 417–446). New York: Plenum Press.

Bromley, H. R., & Kirschner-Bromley, V. A. (2007). Are You a Transformational Leader? *Physician Executive, 33*(6), 54–57.

Brown, K. W., Ryan, R. M., & Creswell, J. D. (2007). Mindfulness Theoretical foundations and evidence for its Salutary Effects. *Psychological Inquiry, 18*(4), 211–237.

Browning, D. S. (1980). *Pluralism and personality: William James and some contemporary cultures of psychology.* Lewisburg, PA: Bucknell University Press.

Budner, S. (1962). Intolerance of ambiguity as a personality variable. *Journal of Personality, 30*(1), 29–50.

Burns, J. M. (1978). *Leadership.* New York: Harper and Row.

Cable, D. M., & Judge, T. A. (1994). Pay preferences and job search decisions: A person–organization fit perspective. *Personnel Psychology, 47*(2), 317–348.

Callan, V. J., Terry, D. J., & Schweitzer, R. (1994). Coping resources, coping strategies and adjustment to organizational change: Direct of buffering effects? *Work and Stress, 8*(4), 372–383.

Cameron, J. E. (1999). Social identity and the pursuit of possible selves: Implications for the psychological well-being of university students. *Group Dynamics: Theory, Research, and Practice, 3*(3), 179–189.

Carole, W., & Tavris, C. (1996). *Psychology.* New York, NY: HarperCollins.

Carr, A. (1999). The psychodynamics of organisation change: Identity and the "reading" of emotion and emotionality in a process of change. *Journal of Managerial Psychology, 14*(7/8), 573–585.

Carr, A. (2001). Understanding emotion and emotionality in a process of change. *Journal of Organizational Change Management, 14*(5), 421–434.

Carskadon, T. G. (1979). Clinical and counseling aspects of the Myers-Briggs Type Indicator: A research review. *Research in Psychological Type, 2*(4), 2–31.

Carter, R. (2008). *Multiplicity: The new science of personality.* London, UK: Little Brown.

Cattell, R. B., Boyle, G. J., & Chant, D. (2002). Enriched behavioral prediction equation and its impact on structured learning and the dynamic calculus. *Psychological Review, 109*(1), 202–205.

Cerasoli, C. P., Nicklin, J. M., & Ford, M. T. (2014). Intrinsic Motivation and Extrinsic Incentives Jointly Predict Performance: A 40-Year Meta-Analysis. *Psychological Bulletin, 140*(4), 980–1008.

Chen, J., & Wang, L. (2007). Locus of control and the three components of commitment to change. *Personality and Individual Differences, 42*(3), 503–512.

Chong, V. K., & Eggleton, I. R. C. (2003). The decision-facilitating role of management accounting systems on managerial performance: the influence of locus of control and task uncertainty. *Advances in Accounting, 20,* 165–197.

Chuck, C. (2007). Placing our assumptions at risk: Pathway to changing the culture of the community college. *Community College Journal of Research and Practice*, *31*(3), 217–229. https://doi.org/10.1080/10668920600859731

Claxton, G. (1994). *Noises from the darkroom: The science and mystery of the mind*. London, UK: Aquarian.

Cleveland, J. N., & Murphy, K. R. (1992). Analyzing performance appraisal as goal-directed behavior. In G. Ferris & K. Rowland (Eds.), *Research in personnel and human resources management* (pp. 121–185). Greenwich, CT: JAI Press.

Cobb-Clark, D. A., & Schurer, S. (2013). Two economists' musings on the stability of locus of control. *The Economic Journal*, *123*(570), F358–F400.

Collingwood, H. (2001). Leadership's first commandment: know thyself. *Harvard Business Review*, *79*(11), 8.

Connor-Smith, J. K., & Flachsbart, C. (2007). Relations between personality and coping: A meta-analysis. *Journal of Personality and Social Psychology*, *93*(6), 1080–1107.

Costa, P. T., & McCrae, R. (1985). *The NEO PI personality inventory*. Odessa, FL: Psychological Assessment Resources.

Costa, P. T., & McCrae, R. R. (1992). Four ways five factors are basic. *Personality and Individual Differences*, *13*(6), 653–665.

Cross, S. E., & Markus, H. (1994). Self-schemas, possible selves, and competent performance. *Journal of Educational Psychology*, *86*(3), 423–438.

Davito, A. (1985). A review of the Myers-Brigs type indicator. In J. Mitchell (Ed.), *Ninth mental measurement yearbook*. Lincoln, NE: University of Nebraska Press.

Day, D. V. (2001). Leadership development: A review in context. *The Leadership Quarterly*, *11*(4), 581–613.

de Board, R. (1978). *The Psychoanalysis of Organisations*. London: Tavistock Publications.

de Board, R. (1983). *Counselling Skills*. Gower Publishing: Aldershot, US.

Deci, E. L. (1976). The hidden costs of rewards. *Organizational Dynamics*, *4*(3), 61–72.

Deci, E. L., & Ryan, R. M. (2010). *Self-Determination*. New York: John Wiley & Sons, Inc.

Diener, E. (1984). Subjective well-being. *Psychological Bulletin*, *95*(3), 542–575.

Diener, E. (2000). Subjective well-being: the science of happiness and a proposal for a national index. *American Psychologist*, *55*(1), 34–43.

Dominé, V. H. (2012). *The Illusion of Control in Leadership Development: The Goals and Fears of INSEAD GEMBA Participants*. INSEAD.

Donald, G. G., & Pierce, J. L. (1998). Self-esteem and self-efficacy within the organizational context: An empirical examination. *Group & Organization Management*, *23*(1), 48–70.

Drath, W. H. (1990). Managerial strengths and weaknesses as functions of the development of personal meaning. *Journal of Applied Behavioral Science*, *26*(4), 483–499.

Duffy, M. K., Ganster, D. C., & Shaw, J. D. (1998). Positive affectivity and negative outcomes: The role of tenure and job satisfaction. *Journal of Applied Psychology, 83*(6), 950–959.

Dunning, D. (2006). Strangers to ourselves. *The Psychologist, 19*(10), 603.

Dweck, C. S. (2006). *Mindset: The new psychology of success.* New York: Random House.

Eigel, K. M. (1998). *Leader effectiveness: A constructive-developmental view and investigation.* Athens: University of Georgia.

Ellis, A. L., & Fooshee, S. G. (1992). The Effect of Experience on the Goal-Setting Behavior of Type A and Type B Individuals. *Basic & Applied Social Psychology, 13*(4), 415–425.

English, H. B., & English, A. C. (1958). *A Comprehensive Dictionary of Psychological and Psychoanalytic Terms.* New York: Longmans, Green.

Erhard, W., Jensen, M. C., & Granger, K. (2011). *Introduction to Being a Leader and the Effective Exercise of Leadership: An Ontological Model (PDF File of PowerPoint Slides)* (Harvard Business School Negotiation, Organizations and Markets Unit, Research Paper Series No. 09–124). Retrieved from http://www.ssrn.com/link/HBS-NOM-Unit.html

Erikson, M. G. (2007). The Meaning of the Future: Toward a More Specific Definition of Possible Selves. *Review of General Psychology, 11*(4), 348–358.

Evans, J. S. B. T. (1989). *Bias in human reasoning: Causes and consequences.* Hillsdale, NJ: Erlbaum.

Eysenck, H. J. (1992). Four ways five factors are not basic. *Personality and Individual Differences, 13*(6), 667–673.

Feather, N. T. (1995). Values, Valences, and Choice: The Influence of Values on the Perceived Attractiveness and Choice of Alternatives. *Journal of Personality and Social Psychology, 68*(6), 1135–1151.

Feldman Barrett, L. (2004). Feelings or words? Understanding the content in self-report ratings of experienced emotion. *Journal of Personality and Social Psychology, 87*(2), 266–281.

Ferreira, M. B., Garcia-Marques, L., Sherman, S. J., & Sherman, J. W. (2006). Automatic and controlled components of judgment and decision making. *Journal of Personality and Social Psychology, 91*(5), 797–813.

Fineman, S. (1993a). Introduction. In S. Fineman (Ed.), *Emotion in organizations* (pp. 1–8). London, UK: Sage Publications.

Fineman, S. (1993b). Organizations as emotional arenas. In S. Fineman (Ed.), *Emotion in Organizations* (pp. 9–35). London, UK: Sage Publications.

Fingarette, H. (2000). *Self-Deception.* London, UK: University of California Press.

Fleeson, W., & Gallagher, P. (2009). The implications of big-five standing for the distribution of trait manifestation in behavior: Fifteen experience-sampling studies and a meta-analysis. *Journal of Personality and Social Psychology, 97*(6), 1097–1114.

Flynn, F. J. (2005). Having an Open Mind: The Impact of Openness to Experience on Interracial Attitudes and Impression Formation. *Journal of Personality and Social Psychology, 88*(5), 816–826.

Fraley, R. C., & Roberts, B. W. (2005). Patterns of continuity: A dynamic model for conceptualizing the stability of individual differences in psychological constructs across the life course. *Psychological Review, 112*(1), 60–74.

French, R. (2001). Negative capability: Managing the confusing uncertainties of change. *Journal of Organizational Change Management, 14*(5), 480–492.

French, R., & Vince, R. (1999). *Group relations, management, and organization.* Oxford: Oxford University Press.

Friedlander, F., & Walton, E. (1964). Positive and negative motivations toward work. *Administrative Science Quarterly, 9*(2), 194–207.

Friedman, M. D., & Rosenman, R. H. (1974). *Type A behavior and your heart.* New York, NY: Knopf.

Frijda, N. H. (2000). The psychologists' point of view. In M. Lewis & J. M. Haviland-Jones (Eds.), *Handbook of emotions* (2nd ed., pp. 59–74). New York: The Guilford Press.

Frisch, M. B. (2006). *Quality of life therapy: Applying a life satisfaction approach to positive psychology and cognitive therapy.* New York: Wiley.

Funder, D. C. (1997). *The personality puzzle.* New York: Norton.

Furnham, A. (1996). The big five versus the big four: The relationship between the Myers-Briggs Type Indicator (MBTI) and NEO-PI five factor model of personality. *Personality and Individual Differences, 21*(2), 303–307.

Furnham, A., & Cheng, H. (2016). Childhood intelligence, self-esteem, early trait neuroticism and behaviour adjustment as predictors of locus of control in teenagers. *Personality and Individual Differences, 95,* 178–182.

Gabriel, Y. (1999). Beyond happy families: A critical reevaluation of the control-resistance-identity triangle. *Human Relations, 52*(2), 179–203.

Gagné, M., & Deci, E. L. (2005). Self-determination theory and work motivation. *Journal of Organizational Behavior, 26*(4), 331–362.

Gardner, W. L., & Avolio, B. J. (1998). The charismatic relationship: A dramaturgical perspective. *Academy of Management Review, 23*(1), 32–58.

Gecas, V. (1982). The Self-Concept. *Annual Review of Sociology, 8,* 1–33.

George, M. A. (1956). Information theory. *Scientific American, 195*(2), 42–46.

Gilbert, P., & Choden. (2013). *Mindful Compassion.* London, UK: Constable and Robinson.

Gist, M. E., & Mitchell, T. R. (1992). Self-efficacy: A theoretical analysis of its determinants and malleability. *Academy of Management Review, 17*(2), 183–211.

Goffman, E. (1959). *The presentation of self in everyday life.* Garden City, NY: Doubleday.

Goleman, D. (1985). *Vital Lies, Simple Truths: The Psychology of Self-Deception*. New York: Simon and Schuster.

Goleman, D. (1996). *Emotional intelligence: Why it can matter more than IQ*. London, UK: Bloomsbury Publishing.

Goleman, D. (1997). *Vital Lies, Simple Truths: The Psychology of Self-Deception*. London, UK: Bloomsbury.

Goleman, D. (2004). What makes a leader? *Harvard Business Review*, 82(1), 82–91.

Graen, G. B., & Uhl-Bien, M. (1995). Relationship-based approach to leadership: Development of leader-member exchange (LMX) theory of leadership over 25 years: Applying a multi-level multi-domain perspective. *The Leadership Quarterly*, 6(2), 219–247.

Grant, A. M., Gino, F., & Hofmann, D. A. (2010). The hidden advantages of quiet bosses. *Harvard Business Review*, 88(12), 28.

Greenwald, A. G. (1988). A social-cognitive account of the self's development. In D. K. Lapsley & F. C. Power (Eds.), *Self, ego, and identity: Integrative approaches* (pp. 30–42). New York: Springer-Verlag.

Greenwald, A. G., Banaji, M. R., Rudman, L. A., Farnham, S. D., Nosek, B. A., & Mellott, D. S. (2002). A unified theory of implicit attitudes, stereotypes, self-esteem, and self-concept. *Psychological Review*, 109(1), 3–25.

Greenwald, A. G., & Pratkanis, A. R. (1984). The self. In R. S. J. Wyer & T. K. Srull (Eds.), *Handbook of social cognition* (pp. 129–178). Hillsdale, NJ: Erlbaum.

Grint, K. (2005). *Leadership: Limits and possibilities*. Basingstoke, Hampshire: Palgrave Macmillan.

Guy, C. (2005). *An intelligent look at emotional intelligence*. London, UK: ATL.

Hafenbrack, A. C. (2014). State Temporal Focus in Organizations and Mindfulness Meditation as an On-The-Spot Intervention. In *Annual meeting of the Academy of Management*. Philadelphia, PA.

Haidt, J. (2006). *The Happiness Hypothesis*. London, UK: Arrow Books.

Hall, D. T. (2004). Self-awareness, identity, and leader development. In D. Day, S. Zaccaro, & S. Halpin (Eds.), *Leader development for transforming organizations — Growing leaders for tomorrow*. (pp. 153–170). New York: Lawrence Erlbaum Associates.

Hasegawa, B. A. (2004). The teacher leader role shift: A constructive-developmental study of teacher leaders' experiences of role transition and authority relationships. Dissertation Abstracts International, 64, 08A. (UMI No. 3100144). *Dissertation Abstracts International*, 64(08A).

Hayes, T. L., Roehm, H. A., & Castellano, J. P. (1994). Personality correlates of success in total quality manufacturing. *Journal of Business and Psychology*, 8(4), 397–411.

Heather, C. E. (1995). Some comments on a factor analysis of the 16PF and NEO Personality Inventory – Revised. *Psychological Reports*, 77(3), 1307–1311.

Heifetz, R. A. (1994). *Leadership without easy answers.* Cambridge: The Belknap Press of Harvard University Press.

Heifetz, R. A., Linsky, M., & Grashow, A. (2009). *The Practice of Adaptive Leadership: Tools and Tactics for Changing Your Organization and the World.* Boston: Harvard Business Press.

Heilbrun Jr, A. B., & Friedberg, E. B. (1988). Type A personality, self-control, and vulnerability to stress. *Journal of Personality Assessment, 52*(3), 420–433.

Held, B. S. (2004). The negative side of positive psychology. *Journal of Humanistic Psychology, 44*(1), 9–46.

Helsing, D., & Howell, A. (2014). Understanding Leadership from the Inside Out: Assessing Leadership Potential Using Constructive-Developmental Theory. *Journal of Management Inquiry, 23*(2), 186–204.

Hendrix, J. S. (2015). *Unconscious Thought in Philosophy and Psychoanalysis.* United Kingdom: Palgrave Macmillan.

Herzberg, F. (1959). *The Motivation to Work.* New York: John Wiley and Sons.

Herzberg, F., Mausner, B., & Snyderman, B. B. (2009). *The Motivation to work.* New Jersey: Transaction Publisher.

Heyman, G. D., & Dweck, C. S. (1998). Children's Thinking about Traits: Implications for Judgments of the Self and Others. *Child Development, 64*(2), 391–403.

Hicks, L. E. (1984). Conceptual and empirical analysis of some assumptions of an explicitly typological theory. *Journal of Personality and Social Psychology, 46*(5), 1118–1131.

Hogan, J., & Holland, B. (2003). Using Theory to Evaluate Personality and Job Performance Relations: A Socioanalytic Perspective. *Journal of Applied Psychology, 88*(1), 100–112.

Holahan, C. J., & Moos, R. H. (1987). Personal and contextual determinants of coping strategies. *Journal of Personality and Social Psychology, 52*(5), 946–955.

Hoover, J. D., Giambatista, R. C., Sorenson, R. L., & Bommer, W. C. (2010). Assessing the effectiveness of whole person learning pedagogy in skill acquisition. *Academy of Management Learning & Education, 9*(2), 192–203.

House, R. J., & Aditya, R. N. (1997). The social scientific study of leadership: Quo Vadis? *Journal of Management, 23*(3), 409–473.

Hudson, P. (2014). The 25 things that people with Type A personalities do. Retrieved September 22, 2017, from http://elitedaily.com/life/motivation/the-25-things-that-people-with-type-a-personalities-do/

Hultman, K. (2006). *Values-driven change: Strategies and tools for long-term success.* Lincoln, NE: iUniverse.

Huy, Q. N. (2002). Emotional balancing of organizational continuity and radical change: The contribution of middle managers. *Administrative Science Quarterly, 47*(1), 31–69.

Hyatt, T. A., & Prawitt, D. F. (2001). Does congruence between audit structure and auditors' locus of control affect job performance? *The Accounting Review, 76*(2), 263–274.

Ibarra, H. (2007). *Identity Transitions: Possible selves, liminality and the dynamics of voluntary career change* (Working Paper 2007/31/OB). Fontainebleau, France.

Ibarra, H., & Petriglieri, J. L. (2010). Identity work and play. *Journal of Organizational Change Management, 23*(1), 10–25.

Iida, M., Shrout, P. E., Laurenceau, J. P., & Bolger, N. (2012). Using diary methods in psychological research. In H. Cooper, P. M. Camic, D. L. Long, A. T. Panter, D. Rindskopf, & K. J. Sher (Eds.), *APA handbook of research methods in psychology, Vol. 1: Foundations, planning, measures, and psychometrics* (pp. 277–305). Washington DC, US: American Psychological Association.

Inglehart, M. R., Markus, H., & Brown, D. R. (1988). The effects of possible selves on academic achievement: A panel study. In *International Congress of Psychology*. Sydney, Australia.

Ireland, M. E., Hepler, J., Li, H., & Albarracín, D. (2014). Neuroticism and attitudes toward action in 19 countries. *Journal of Personality, 83*(3), 243–250.

Israel, B. A., House, J. S., Schurman, S. J., Heaney, C. A., & Mero, R. P. (1989). The relation of personal resources, participation, influence, interpersonal relationships and coping strategies to occupational stress, job strains and health: A multivariate analysis. *Work & Stress, 3*(2), 163–194.

James, W. (2007). *The Principles of Psychology*. New York: Cosimo Inc.

Jeffrey, S., & Gladding, R. (2011). *You are not your brain: The 4-step solution for changing bad habits, ending unhealthy thinking, and taking control of your life*. New York: Avery.

Jenny, W. (1996). *Changes of mind: A holonomic theory of the evolution of consciousness*. Albany, NJ: University of New York Press.

Johnson, J. A. (1997). Seven social performance scales for the California Psychological Inventory. *Human Performance, 10*(1), 1–30.

Judge, T. A., Bono, J. E., Ilies, R., & Gerhardt, M. W. (2002). Personality and leadership: A qualitative and quantitative review. *Journal of Applied Psychology, 87*(4), 765–780.

Judge, T. A., Higgins, C. A., Thoresen, C. J., & Barrick, M. R. (1999). The Big Five personality traits, general mental ability, and career success across the life span. *Personnel Psychology, 52*(3), 621–652.

Judge, T. A., & Ilies, R. (2002). Relationship of personality to performance motivation: A meta-analytic review. *Journal of Applied Psychology, 87*(4), 797–807.

Judge, T. A., & Locke, E. A. (1993). The Effect of Dysfunctional Thought Processes on Subjective Well-Being and Job Satisfaction. *Journal of Applied Psychology, 78*(3), 475–490.

Judge, T. A., Simon, L. S., Hurst, C., & Kelley, K. (2014). What I Experienced Yesterday Is Who I Am Today: Relationship of Work Motivations and Behaviors to Within-Individual Variation in the Five-Factor Model of Personality. *Journal of Applied Psychology, 99*(2), 199–221.

Judge, T. A., Thoresen, C. J., Pucik, V., & Welbourne, T. M. (1999). Managerial coping with organizational change: A dispositional perspective. *Journal of Applied Psychology*, *84*(1), 107–122.

Kahneman, D. (2003). A perspective on judgment and choice: mapping bounded rationality. *American Psychologist*, *58*(9), 697–720.

Kahneman, D. (2011). *Thinking Fast and Slow*. London, UK: Allen Lane.

Kahneman, D., & Frederick, S. (2002). Representativeness revisited: Attribute substitution in intuitive judgment. In T. Gilovich, D. Griffin, & D. Kahneman (Eds.), *Heuristics & Biases: The Psychology of Intuitive Judgment* (pp. 49–81). New York: Cambridge University Press.

Kahneman, D., & Tversky, A. (1979). *Judgment under uncertainty: Heuristics and biases*. New York: Cambridge University Press.

Kaplan, S., Bradley, J. C., Luchman, J. N., & Haynes, D. (2009). On the role of positive and negative affectivity in job performance: A meta-analytic investigation. *Journal of Applied Psychology*, *94*(1), 162–176.

Katz, D., Maccoby, N., Gurin, G., & Floor, L. G. (1951). *Productivity, supervision and morale among rail road workers*. Ann Arbor: Institute for Social Research, University of Michigan.

Kegan, R. (1982). *The Evolving Self: Problem and Process in Human Development*. Cambridge, MA: Harvard University Press.

Kegan, R. (1994). *In over Our Heads: The Mental Demands of Modern Life*. Cambridge, MA: Harvard University Press.

Kegan, R. (2000). What "form" transforms?: A constructive-developmental approach to transformative learning. In K. Illeris (Ed.), *Contemporary Theories of Learning. Learning theorists ... in their own words* (pp. 35–52). Oxford, UK: Routledge.

Kegan, R., & Lahey, L. (2001a). The real reason people won't change. *Harvard Business Review*, *79*(10), 85–92.

Kegan, R., & Lahey, L. (2001b). *The Way We Talk Can Change the Way We Work: Seven Languages for Transformation*. Jossey-Bass: San Francisco, CA.

Kegan, R., & Lahey, L. (2009). *Immunity to change: How to overcome it and unlock the potential in yourself and in your organization*. Boston: Harvard Business Press.

Kelly, G. A. (1955). *The Psychology of Personal Constructs*. New York: Norton.

Kets de Vries, M., & Korotov, K. (2007). Creating transformational executive education programs. *Academy of Management Learning and Education*, *6*(3), 375–387.

Kihlstrom, J. F. (1999). The psychological unconscious. In L. R. Pervin & O. John (Eds.), *Handbook of personality* (2nd ed., pp. 424–442). New York: Guilford Press.

Kirk, B. W., & Ryan, R. M. (2003). The benefits of being present: Mindfulness and its role in psychological well-being. *Journal of Personality and Social Psychology*, *84*(4), 822–848.

Kirkpatrick, S. A., & Locke, E. A. (1991). Leadership: Do Traits Matter? *Academy of Management Executive*, 5(2), 48–60.

Krippner, S., Pitchford, D., & Davies, J. (2012). *Post-traumatic stress disorder: Biographies of disease*. Santa Barbara, CA: Greenwood/ABC-CLIO.

Kudesia, R. S. (2017). Mindfulness as metacognitive practice. *Academy of Management Review*, (ja).

Kuhnert, K. W., & Lewis, P. (1987). Transactional and transformational leadership: A constructive/developmental analysis. *Academy of Management Review*, 12(4), 648–657.

Langer, E. J. (2009). *Counterclockwise: Mindful health and the power of possibility*. New York: Ballantine Books.

Lawler, E. E. I. (1973). *Motivation in work organizations*. Monterrey, CA: Brooks/Cole Publishing Company.

Leary, M. R., Koch, E., & Hechenbleikner, N. (2001). Emotional responses to interpersonal rejection. In M. R. Leary (Ed.), *Interpersonal rejection* (pp. 145–166). New York: Oxford University Press.

Leary, M. R., Tambor, E., Terdal, S., & Downs, D. L. (1999). Self-esteem as an interpersonal monitor: The sociometer hypothesis. In R. Baumeister (Ed.), *The Self in Social Psychology* (pp. 87–104). Hove: Psychology Press.

LeDoux, J. E. (1992). Emotion and the amygdala. In J. P. Aggleton (Ed.), *The amygdala: Neurobiological aspects of emotion, memory, and mental dysfunction* (pp. 339–351). New York, NY, US: Wiley-Liss.

Lee-Baggley, D., Preece, M., & DeLongis, A. (2005). Coping with interpersonal stress: Role of Big Five traits. *Journal of Personality*, 73(5), 1141–1180.

Lee, G. (2010). The psychodynamic approach to coaching. In E. Cox, T. Bachkirova, & D. Clutterbuck (Eds.), *The complete handbook of coaching* (pp. 23–36). London, UK: Sage Publications.

Lefcourt, H. M. (2013). Locus of Control. In J. P. Robinson, P. R. Shaver, & L. S. Wrightsman (Eds.), *Measures of Personality and Social Psychological Attitudes* (pp. 413–499). San Diego, CA: Academic Press.

Leonard, D., & Straus, S. (1997). Putting Your Company's Whole Brain to Work. *Harvard Business Review*, 74(4), 110–121.

Loevinger, J. (1976). *Ego development: Conceptions and theories*. San Francisco, CA: Jossey-Bass Publishers.

Loevinger, J. (1987). *Paradigms of personality*. New York: Freeman.

Lofland, J., & Lofland, L. H. (2006). *Analyzing social settings*. Belmont, CA: Wadsworth Publishing Company.

Ludeman, K., & Erlandson, E. (2006). *Alpha male syndrome*. Boston, MA: Harvard Business School Press.

Ludeman, K., & Erlandson, E. (2007). Channeling alpha male leaders. *Leader to Leader*, 44(2), 38–44.

Luthans, F. (2002). The need for and meaning of positive organizational behavior. *Journal of Organizational Behavior*, 23(6), 695–706.

Luthans, F., & Avolio, B. J. (2003). Authentic leadership: A positive development approach. In K. S. Cameron, J. E. Dutton, & R. E. Quinn (Eds.), *Positive organizational scholarship: Foundations of a new discipline* (pp. 241–261). San Francisco, CA: Berrett-Koehler.

MacKay, D. G. (1981). The problem of rehearsal or mental practice. *Journal of Motor Behavior, 13*(4), 274–285.

Maehr, M. L., & Videbeck, R. (1968). Predisposition to risk and persistence under varying reinforcement-success schedules. *Journal of Personality and Social Psychology, 9*(1), 96–100.

Mahajan, E., & Rastogi, R. (2011). Psychological Wellbeing of Students with Type A and Type B Personalities. *The IUP Journal of Organizational Behavior, X*(1), 57–74.

Malim, T., & Birch, A. (1998). *Introductory psychology*. London: Macmillan Press Ltd.

Mann, R. D. (1959). A review of the relationships between personality and performance in small groups. *Psychological Bulletin, 56*(4), 241–270.

Markus, H. (1990). Unresolved issues of self-representation. *Cognitive Therapy and Research, 14*(2), 241–253.

Markus, H., & Nurius, P. (1986). Possible selves. *American Psychologist, 41*(9), 954–969.

Markus, H., & Ruvolo, A. (1989). Possible selves: Personalized representations of goals. In L. A. Pervin (Ed.), *Goal concepts in personality and social psychology* (pp. 211–241). Hillsdale, NJ: Erlbaum.

Markus, H., & Wurf, E. (1987). The dynamic self-concept: A social psychological perspective. *Annual Review of Psychology, 38*(1), 299–337.

Martha, B. A. (1976). Values-A Necessary but Neglected Ingredient of Motivation. *Academy of Management Review, 1*(4), 15–23.

Maslow, A. H. (1954). *Motivation and personality*. New York: Harper and Row.

Matlin, M. W. (1995). *Psychology* (2nd ed.). Fort Worth, TX: Harcourt Brace College Publishers.

Matthews, K. A. (1982). Psychological perspectives on the Type A behavior pattern. *Psychological Bulletin, 91*(2), 293–323.

Matthews, K. A., & Saal, F. E. (1978). Relationship of the type A coronary-prone behavior pattern to achievement, power, and affiliation motives. *Psychosomatic Medicine, 40*(8), 631–636.

Mayer, J. D., & Salovey, P. (1997). What is emotional intelligence? In P. Salovey & D. J. Sluyter (Eds.), *Emotional development and emotional intelligence: Educational implications* (pp. 3–31). New York: Basic Books.

Mayo, M., Kakarika, M., Pastor, J. C., & Brutus, S. (2012). Aligning or Inflating Your Leadership Self-Image? A Longitudinal Study of Responses to Peer Feedback in MBA Teams. *Academy of Management Learning & Education, 11*(4), 631–652.

McAuliffe, G. (2006). The evolution of professional competence. In C. Hoare (Ed.), *Handbook of adult development and learning* (pp. 476–496). New York: Oxford University Press.

McAvoy, J., & Butler, T. (2005). A paradox of the change to User Stories: The application of the theory of Competing Commitments. In *13th European Conference on Information Systems, University of Regensburg, Germany*.

McCall, M. W. J. (2009). Every strength a weakness and other caveats. In R. B. Kaiser (Ed.), *The Perils of Accentuating the Positive* (pp. 41–56). Tulsa, OK: Hogan Press.

McCauley, C. D., Drath, W. H., Palus, C. J., O'Connor, P. M. G., & Baker, B. A. (2006). The use of constructive-developmental theory to advance the understanding of leadership. *The Leadership Quarterly, 17*(6), 634–653.

McCrae, R. R., & Costa, P. T. (1986). Personality, coping, and coping effectiveness in an adult sample. *Journal of Personality, 54*(2), 385–404.

McCrae, R. R., & Costa, P. T. (1989). Reinterpreting the Myers-Briggs Type Indicator from the perspective of the five-factor model of personality. *Journal of Personality, 57*(1), 17–40.

McCrae, R. R., & John, O. P. (1992). An introduction to the Five-Factor Model and its applications. *Journal of Personality, 60*(2), 175–215.

Menzies, I. E. (1960). A case study in the functioning of social systems as a defence against anxiety. *Human Relations, 13*(2), 95–121.

Miller, E. J., & Rice, A. K. (1967). *Systems of Organization: The control of task and sentient boundaries*. London: Tavistock Publications.

Mondillon, L., Niedenthal, P. M., Brauer, M., Rohmann, A., Dalle, N., & Uchida, Y. (2005). Beliefs about power and its relation to emotional experience: A comparison of Japan, France, Germany and the United States. *Personality and Social Psychology Bulletin, 31*(8), 1122–1132.

Mruk, C. J. (2006). *Self-esteem Research, Theory and Practice: Toward a Positive Psychology of Self-esteem* (3rd ed.). New York: Springer Publishing Company.

Mueller, C. M., & Dweck, C. S. (1998). Praise for Intelligence Can Undermine Children's Motivation and Performance. *Journal of Personality and Social Psychology, 75*(1), 33–52.

Mumford, M. D., Helton, W. B., Decker, B. P., Connelly, S., & Van Doorn, J. R. (2003). Values and beliefs related to ethical decisions. *Teaching Business Ethics, 7*, 139–170.

Myers, I. B., & McCaulley, M. H. (1985). *Manual: A guide to the development and use of the Myers-Briggs type indicator*. Palo Alto, CA.: Consulting Psychologists Press.

Nelson, A., Cooper, C. L., & Jackson, P. R. (1995). Uncertainty amidst change: The impact of privatization on employee job satisfaction and well-being. *Journal of Occupational and Organizational Psychology, 68*(1), 57–71.

Norretranders, T. (1998). *The user illusion: Cutting consciousness down to size*. New York: Viking.

O'Brien, K. (2013). The courage to change: Adaptation from the inside-out. In S. Moser & M. Boykoff (Eds.), *Successful Adaptation to Climate Change: Linking Science and Practice in Managing Climate Change Impacts* (pp. 306–320). London, UK: Routledge.

Oldham, M., & Kleiner, B. H. (1990). Understanding the nature and use of defense mechanisms in organisational life. *Journal of Managerial Psychology*, 5(5), 1–4.

Olson, E. E. (1990). The transcendent function in organizational change. *The Journal of Applied Behavioural Science*, 26(1), 69–81.

Oreg, S., Bayast, M., Vakola, M., Arciniega, L., Armenakis, A. Barkauskiene, R., & et al. (2008). Dispositional resistance to change: Measurement equivalence and the link to personal values across 17 nations. *Journal of Applied Psychology*, 93(4), 935–944.

Organ, D. W., & Greene, C. N. (1974). Role ambiguity, locus of control and work satisfaction. *Journal of Applied Psychology*, 59(1), 101–102.

Oyserman, D., Bybee, D., & Terry, K. (2006). Possible selves and academic outcomes: How and when possible selves impel action. *Journal of Personality and Social Psychology*, 91(1), 181–204.

Oyserman, D., & Markus, H. (1990). Possible selves and delinquency. *Journal of Personality and Social Psychology*, 59(1), 112–125.

Palmer, B., Walls, M., Burgess, Z., & Stough, C. (2000). Emotional intelligence and effective leadership. *Leadership and Organization Development Journal*, 22(1), 5–10.

Passmore, J., Peterson, D., & Freire, T. (2012). *The Wiley-Blackwell Handbook of the Psychology of Coaching and Mentoring*. New York: John Wiley & Sons.

Parks, L., & Guay, R. P. (2009). Personality, values, and motivation. *Personality and Individual Differences*, 47(7), 675–684. https://doi.org/10.1016/j.paid.2009.06.002

Parrott, W. G. (2002). The functional utility of negative emotions. In L. F. Barrett & P. Salovey (Eds.), *The wisdom in feeling: Psychological processes in emotional intelligence* (pp. 341–359). New York: The Guilford Press.

Penney, L. M., & Spector, P. E. (2005). Job stress, incivility, and counterproductive work behavior (CWB): The moderating role of negative affectivity. *Journal of Organizational Behavior*, 26(7), 777–796.

Peterson, C. (2000). The future of optimism. *American Psychologist*, 55(1), 44–55.

Peterson, C., & Seligman, M. E. P. (2004). *Character Strengths and Virtues: A Handbook and Classification*. New York: American Psychological Association.

Petriglieri, G., & Stein, M. (2012). The unwanted self: Projective identification in leaders' identity work. *Organization Studies*, 33(9), 1217–1235.

Petriglieri, G., Wood, J. D., & Petriglieri, J. L. (2011). Up Close and Personal: Developing Foundations for Leader Development through Personalization of Management Learning. *Academy of Management Learning and Education*, 10(3), 430–450.

Pinder, C. C. (2014). *Work motivation in organizational behavior.* New York, NY: Psychology Press.

Pines, H. A., & Julian, J. W. (1972). Effects of task and social demands on locus of control differences in information processing. *Journal of Personality, 40*(3), 407–416.

Pink, D. H. (2009). *Drive: The surprising truth about what motivates us.* New York: Riverhead Books.

Plous, S. (1993). *The psychology of judgment and decision making.* New York: McGraw-Hill.

Prati, L., Douglas, C., Ferris, G., Ammeter, A., & Buckley, M. (2003). Emotional intelligence, leadership effectiveness, and team outcomes. *International Journal of Organizational Analysis, 11*(1), 21–40.

Raudsepp, E. (1990). Are you flexible enough to succeed? *Manage, 42*(2), 6.

Richardson, A. (1967). Mental practice: A review and discussion, Part I. *Research Quarterly, 38*(1), 95–107.

Robbins, H., & Finley, M. (1998). *Why change doesn't work.* London: Orion Publishing.

Robertson, I. (2000). Conscientiousness and managerial performance. *Journal of Occupational & Organizational Psychology, 73*(2), 171–180.

Robins, R. W., Hendin, H. M., & Trzesniewski, K. H. (2001). Measuring Global Self-Esteem: Construct Validation of a Single-Item Measure and the Rosenberg Self-Esteem Scale. *Personality and Social Psychology Bulletin, 27*(2), 151–161.

Rokeach, M. (1973). *The nature of human values.* New York: Free Press.

Rooke, D., & Torbert, W. R. (1998). Organizational transformation as a function of CEOs' developmental stage. *Organization Development Journal, 16*(1), 11–28.

Rosenman, R. H., Friedman, M., Strauss, R., Wurm, M., Kositichok, R., Haan, W., & Werthessen, N. T. (1964). A predictive study of coronary heart disease: The Western Collaborative Group Study. *Jama, 189*(1), 15–22.

Rothmann, S., & Coetzer, E. P. (2003). The big five personality dimensions and job performance. *SA Journal of Industrial Psychology, 29*(1), 68–74.

Rotter, J. B. (1966). Generalized expectancies for internal versus external control of reinforcement. Psychological Monographs, 80(1, Whole No. 609). *Psychological Monographs: General and Applied, 80*(1), 1–28.

Ryan, R. M., & Deci, E. L. (2000). Intrinsic and Extrinsic Motivations: Classic Definitions and New Directions. *Contemporary Educational Psychology, 25*(1), 54–67.

Rycroft, C. (1995). *A Critical Dictionary of Psychoanalysis* (2nd ed.). Harmondsworth: Penguin Books.

Rydell, S. T. (1966). Tolerance of ambiguity and semantic differential ratings. *Psychological Reports, 19*(3), 1303–1312.

Saggino, A., Cooper, C., & Kline, P. (1999). A confirmatory factor analysis of the Myers-Briggs Type Indicator. *Personality and Individual Differences, 30*(1), 3–9.

Salgado, J. F. (1997). The five-factor model of personality and job performance in the European Community. *Journal of Applied Psychology*, *82*(1), 30–43.

Sandler, C. (2011). *Executive Coaching: A psychodynamic approach*. Berkshire, UK: Open University Press.

Schlitz, M. M., Vieten, C., & Miller, E. M. (2010). Worldview Transformation and the Development of Social Consciousness. *Journal of Consciousness Studies*, *7*(7/8), 18–36.

Schouten, J. W. (1991). Selves in transition: Symbolic consumption in personal rites of passages and identity reconstruction. *Journal of Consumer Research*, *17*(4), 412–425.

Schunk, D. H. (1983). Developing children's self-efficacy and skills: The roles of social comparative information and goal setting. *Educational Psychology*, *8*(1), 76–86.

Schwenk, C. H. (1986). Information, cognitive biases, and commitment to a course of action. *Academy of Management Review*, *11*(2), 298–310.

Schwartz, M., & Begley, S. (2002). *The Mind and the Brain: Neuroplasticity and the Power of Mental Force*. New York: HarperCollins.

Scott-Ladd, B., & Chan, C. C. A. (2004). Emotional intelligence and participation in decision-making: Strategies for promoting organizational learning and change. *Strategic Change*, *13*(2), 95–105.

Seeman, M. (1963). Alienation and social learning in a reformatory. *American Journal of Sociology*, *69*(3), 270–284.

Seligman, M. E. P. (1998a). Building human strengths: psychology's forgotten mission. *APA Monitor*, *29*(1), 2.

Seligman, M. E. P. (1998b). Positive social science. *APA Monitor*, *29*(4), 5.

Shaffakat, S., Otaye, L., Reb, J. M., Chandwani, R., & Vongswasdi, P. (2017). Acting but Not Reacting: Role of Mindfulness in Moderating the PCV–Deviance Relationship. In Academy of Management Proceedings (Vol. 2017, No. 1, p. 17745). Briarcliff Manor, NY 10510: Academy of Management.

Shalom, S. H. (1992). Universals in the content and structure of values: Theoretical advances and empirical tests in 20 countries. In M. P. Zanna (Ed.), *Advances in experimental social psychology* (pp. 1–65). New York: Academic Press.

Shamir, B., & Eilam, G. (2005). "What's your story?" A life-stories approach to authentic leadership development. *Leadership Quarterly*, *16*(3), 395–417.

Shrauger, J. S., & Rosenberg, S. E. (1970). Self-esteem and the effects of success and failure feedback on performance. *Journal of Personality*, *38*(3), 404–417.

Smillie, L. D., Yeo, G. B., Furnham, A. F., & Jackson, C. J. (2006). Benefits of All Work and No Play: The Relationship Between Neuroticism and Performance as a Function of Resource Allocation. *Journal of Applied Psychology*, *91*(1), 139–155.

Smith, C. A., & Kirby, L. D. (2000). Consequences require antecedents: Toward a process model of emotion elicitation. In J. Forgas (Ed.), *Feeling and thinking:*

*The role of affect in social cognition* (pp. 83–106). New York: Cambridge University Press.

Smollan, R. K. (2009). *The Emotional rollercoaster of Organisational Change: Affective Responses to Organisational Change, their Cognitive Antecedents and Behavioural Consequences.* Massey University, Auckland.

Snyder, C. R. (2000). *Handbook of hope*. San Diego, CA: Academic Press.

Solomon, R. C. (2003). *Not passion's slave: Emotions and choice*. New York: Oxford University Press.

Steers, R. M. (1984). *Introduction to Organizational Behavior* (2nd ed.). Glenview, IL: Scott, Foresman.

Stets, J. E., & Burke, P. J. (2000). Identity theory and social identity theory, *Social Psychology Quarterly*, *63*(3), 224–237.

Stewart, W. H., & Roth, P. L. (2001). Risk propensity differences between entrepreneurs and managers: A meta-analytic review. *Journal of Applied Psychology*, *86*(1), 145–153.

Stogdill, R. M. (1948). Personal factors associated with leadership: A survey of the literature. *The Journal of Psychology*, *25*(1), 35–71.

Stogdill, R. M., & Coons, A. E. (1957). *Leader behavior: Its description and measurement*. Oxford, England: Ohio State University, Bureau of Business Research.

Stone, B. (2010, June 14). Settlement Was Paid in Whitman Shoving Incident. *New York Times*.

Stricker, L. J., & Ross, J. (1964). An assessment of some structural properties of the Jungian personality typology. *The Journal of Abnormal and Social Psychology*, *68*(1), 62–71.

Taylor, J. (2012, January). Personal Growth: Motivation: The Drive to Change. *Psychology Today*. Retrieved from http://www.psychologytoday.com/blog/the-power-prime/201201/personal-growth-motivation-the-drive-change

Teoh, H. Y., & Foo, S. L. (1997). Moderating Effects of Tolerance for Ambiguity and Risk-Taking Propensity on the Role Conflict-Perceived Performance Relationship: Evidence From Singaporean Entrepreneurs. *Journal of Business Venturing*, *12*(1), 67–81.

Terracciano, A., Costa, P. T., & McCrae, R. R. (2006). Personality plasticity after age 30. *Personality and Social Psychology Bulletin*, *32*(8), 999–1009.

Tiffany, S. T. (1990). A cognitive model of drug urges and drug-use behavior: role of automatic and nonautomatic processes. *Psychological Review*, *97*(2), 147–168.

Tobacyk, J. J., Livingston, M. M., & Robbins, J. E. (2008). Relationships between Myers-Briggs type indicator measure of psychological type and neo measure of big five personality factors in polish university students: A preliminary cross-cultural comparison. *Psychological Reports*, *103*(2), 588–590.

Tokar, D. M., & Subich, L. M. (1997). Relative contributions of congruence and personality dimensions to job satisfaction. *Journal of Vocational Behavior*, *50*(3), 482–491.

Torbert, W. R. (1987). *Managing the corporate dream: Restructuring for long-term success*. Homewood, IL: Dow Jones-Irwin.

Torbert, W. R. (1991). *The power of balance: Transforming self, society, and scientific inquiry*. Newbury Park, CA: Sage Publications.

Torbert, W. R. (2006). Generating simultaneous personal, team, and organization development. In J. Gallos (Ed.), *Organization Development* (pp. 813–828). San Francisco, CA: Jossey-Bass.

Torbert, W. R., Cook-Greuter, S., Fisher, D., Foldy, E., Gauthier, A., Keeley, K., ... Tran, M. (2004). *Action inquiry: The secret of timely and transforming leadership*. San Francisco, CA: Berrett-Koehler Publishers.

Tsui, J., & Gul, F. A. (1996). Auditors' behaviors in a conflict situation: A research note on the role of locus of control and ethical reasoning. *Accounting, Organizations and Society, 21*(1), 41–51.

Vakola, M., Tsaousis, I., & Nikalaou, I. (2004). The role of emotional intelligence and personality variables on attitudes toward organizational change. *Journal of Managerial Psychology, 19*(2), 88–110.

van den Heuvel, M., Demerouti, E., Schreurs, B. H., Bakker, A. B., & Schaufeli, W. B. (2009). Does meaning-making help during organizational change?: Development and validation of a new scale. *Career Development International, 14*(6), 508–533.

van der Erve, M. (1990). The power of tomorrow's management. *Management Decision, 28*(7), 55–63.

Van Velsor, E., & Drath, W. H. (2004). A lifelong developmental perspective on leader development. In C. D. McCauley & E. Van Velsor (Eds.), *The center for creative leadership handbook of leadership development* (pp. 383–414). San Francisco, CA: Jossey-Bass.

Velsor, E. V., & Leslie, J. B. (1995). Why Executives Derail: Perspectives Across Time and Cultures. *Academy of Management Executive, 9*(4), 62–72.

Vos, J. (2006). *The role of personality and emotions in employee resistance to change*. Rotterdam: Erasmus University.

Wade, J. (1996). *Changes of mind: A holonomic theory of the evolution of consciousness*. Albany, NY: University of New York Press.

Wagner, T., Kegan, R., Lahey, L., Lemons, R. W., Garnier, J., & Helsing, D. (2006). *Change leadership: A practical guide to transforming our schools*. San Francisco, CA: Jossey-Bass.

Ward, R. M., Popson, H. C., & DiPaolo, D. G. (2010). Defining the alpha female: A female leadership measure. *Journal of Leadership & Organizational Studies, 17*(3), 309–320.

Watson, D., & Clark, L. A. (1984). Negative Affectivity: The disposition to experience aversive emotional states. *Psychological Bulletin, 96*(3), 465–490.

Watson, D., & Clark, L. A. (1994a). Emotions, Moods, Traits and Temperament: Conceptual Distinctions and Empirical Findings. In P. Ekman & R. J. Davidson (Eds.), *The Nature of Emotion: Fundamental Questions* (pp. 89–93). New York: Oxford University Press.

Watson, D., & Clark, L. A. (1994b). *Manual for the Positive and Negative Affect Schedule (Expanded Form)* (Unpublished manuscript). Iowa City.

Watson, D., & Clark, L. A. (1997). Extraversion and its positive emotional core. In R. Hogan, J. Johnson, & S. Briggs (Eds.), *Handbook of personality psychology* (pp. 767–793). San Diego, CA: Academic Press.

Wegner, D. M. (1994). Ironic processes of mental control. *Psychological Review*, *101*(1), 34–52.

Weick, K. E. (1995). *Sensemaking in Organizations*. London, UK: Sage Publications.

Westerberg, M., Singh, J., & Häckner, E. (1997). Does the CEO matter? An empirical study of small Swedish firms operating in turbulent environments. *Scandinavian Journal of Management*, *13*(3), 251–270.

Williams, S. L. (2011). Engaging values in international business practice. *Business Horizons*, *54*(4), 315–324.

Wood, J. D., & Petriglieri, G. (2005). Fundamental for a world class leadership programme. In P. Strebel & T. Keys (Eds.), *Mastering executive education: How to combine content with context and emotion* (pp. 364–380). London, UK: Financial Times-Prentice Hall.

Woodman, R. W., & Dewett, T. (2004). Organizationally relevant journeys in individual change. In M. S. Poole & A. H. Van de Ven (Eds.), *Handbook of organizational change and innovation* (pp. 32–49). Oxford, UK: Oxford University Press.

Woodward, I. C., (2017). *Insightfully Aware Leadership – From Aspiration to Practice*. INSEAD Advanced Management Programme Materials Article, Fontainebleau.

Woodward, I. C., & Shaffakat, S. (2014). *Understanding values for insightfully aware leadership* (No. 2014/46/OBH). INSEAD Research Working Paper, Singapore.

Woodward, I. C., & Shaffakat, S. (2016). *Understanding values for insightfully aware leadership* (No. 2016/05/OBH). INSEAD Research Working Paper, Singapore. Retrieved from https://doi.org/10.2139/ssrn.2471492

Woodward, I.C., & Shaffakat, S. (2017). Innovation, leadership and communication intelligence. In N. Pfeffermann & L. Mortara (Eds.), *Strategy and Communication for Innovation* (3rd Edition), Chapter 15, pp. 245–264. Springer International Publishing.

Wurf, E., & Markus, H. (1991). Possible selves and the psychology of personal growth. In D. J. Ozer & J. M. Healy (Eds.), *Perspectives in Personality* (Vol. 3, pp. 39–62). London, UK: Kingsley.

Yammarino, F. J., & Atwater, L. E. (1993). Understanding self-perception accuracy: Implications for human resource management. *Human Resource Management*, *32*(2/3), 231–247.

# Author Index[1]

**A**
Aspinwall, Lisa G., 3, 12
Avolio, Bruce J., 75, 135

**B**
Bachkirova, Tatiana, 4, 22, 24–27, 35, 38, 39, 51–53, 64, 91, 101, 107
Bandura, Albert, 55, 56, 110
Bass, Bernard M., 135
Beechler, Schon, 13, 17
Boyatzis, Richard E., 1n1, 4, 5, 10, 11, 90, 92, 136

**C**
Costa, Paul T., 42, 43, 48, 60, 105, 106, 108

**D**
Deci, Edward L., 66, 67, 112
Dominé, Vincent H., 71–73

**E**
Erikson, Martin G., 27, 28, 30
Erlandson, Eddie, 61

**F**
Freud, Sigmund, 23, 35, 37n7, 69
Friedman, Meyer D., 61

**G**
Gardner, William L., 75
Goleman, Daniel, 9, 10, 38, 53, 75, 109

---

[1] Note: Page numbers followed by 'n' refer to notes.

## H

Heifetz, Ronald A., 1n1, 14, 75, 135
Herzberg, Frederick Irving, 66, 67, 112

## I

Ibarra, Herminia, 6, 29, 30, 135

## J

Judge, Timothy A., 42–44, 47, 51, 57, 57n9, 58, 60, 109–111
Jung, Carl Gustav, 105

## K

Kahneman, Daniel, 23, 24, 58, 105, 107, 111
Kegan, Robert, viii, 4, 5, 13–19, 22, 23, 52, 53, 72, 75, 89, 90, 100–104, 136, 137
Kirkpatrick, Shelley A., 60

## L

Lahey, Lisa Laskow, viii, 4, 5, 14–19, 22, 23, 53, 72, 75, 89, 90, 100–104, 137
Locke, Edwin A., 47, 60
Ludeman, Kate, 61
Luthans, Fred, 12, 75, 135

## M

Mayer, John D., 38, 135
McCall, Morgan W. J., 3, 13
McCrae, Robert R., 42–45, 47, 48, 60, 105, 106, 108
Miller, Eric J., 10

## P

Petriglieri, Gianpiero, 1, 6, 9, 10, 75, 90, 92, 135
Platner, Ernst, 23

## R

Rice, Albert, K., 10
Rosenman, Ray H., 61
Rotter, Julian B., 54, 109
Ryan, Richard M., 66, 67, 112, 137

## S

Salovey, Peter, 38, 135
Seligman, Martin E. P., 4, 12, 75, 136
Shaffakat, Samah, 2, 13, 63, 64, 73, 86, 112, 137
Staudinger, Ursula M., 3, 12

## T

Torbert, William R., 13, 15–17, 100
Tversky, Amos, 58, 111

## W

Woodward, Ian C., 2, 13, 17, 63, 64, 73, 86, 112

# Subject Index[1]

**A**
Anxiety, 35–37, 47, 51, 59, 68, 80, 111, 112, 119, 125

**B**
Behavioral decision theory, 91
Behavioral patterns
  Alpha, 61, 90
  Beta, 61, 90

**C**
Cognitive processing, 90
Consciousness
  subconscious, 23, 37
  unconscious, 2–4, 10, 11n1, 19, 21–30, 41–42, 51–61, 63–69, 89, 90, 101, 112

**D**
Development approaches
  adult mind development, 4, 13–19, 75
  developmental coaching, 4
  immunity to change process, 4, 13–19
  positive leadership, 4, 75
Drive, 5, 9, 23, 45, 54, 55, 60, 68, 69, 109, 125, 129, 131
  achievement motivation, 61, 68

---

[1] Note: Page numbers followed by 'n' refer to notes.

Drivers and Blockers Exploration Tool, 2, 4–6, 13, 19, 65, 71–77, 86, 90, 91, 98, 113, 117–134

**E**
Emotions
  affect; emotional intelligence, 37–40, 58, 75, 76, 135; negative affectivity, 57; negative emotions, 12, 17, 36–38, 44, 47, 57, 72, 80, 108, 110, 119, 125, 130; positive affectivity, 57, 110; positive emotions, 29, 35, 38, 39, 44, 82, 120, 126, 131

**I**
Identity theory, 91
Insightful awareness, 1, 2n2, 9, 11, 13, 92
  insightfully aware leadership development, 87
Intentional change theory (ICT), 4, 5, 10, 11, 90, 136

**L**
Leadership development
  action learning, 92
  coaching, 4n3, 6, 39, 72, 75, 87, 92, 99
  integrated development, 1
  leadership development objectives, 6, 71, 72, 79, 91, 119, 125, 130
  mindfulness, 84, 137
  360 degree leadership assessment, 92
Leadership frameworks, models, approaches and descriptors
  adaptive leadership, 75, 135

authentic leadership, 75, 135
charismatic leadership, 75, 135
leader-member exchange (LMX) theory, 136
positive leadership, 75, 136
traditional leadership, 137
transactional leadership, 136
transformational leadership, 135
values-based leadership, 136
Locus of control
  external locus of control, 54, 55, 109
  internal locus of control, 54, 55, 109

**M**
Mini-selves, 4, 19, 22, 25–27, 69, 91, 107
Motivation
  extrinsic motivator, 4, 19, 24, 25, 61, 65–69, 98, 112
  extrinsic-negative motivator, 68, 98, 112
  extrinsic-positive motivator, 68, 98, 112
  intrinsic motivator, 4, 6, 19, 24, 25, 65–69, 98, 112
  intrinsic-negative motivator, 68, 98
  intrinsic-positive motivator, 68, 98, 112
  negative motivation, 66, 98
  positive motivation, 66, 98, 112

**O**
Ontological Constraints
  amygdala hijacks, 33
  ontological Functional Constraints, 32, 33, 96
  ontological Perceptual Constraints, 32, 33, 95
Orders of mind

self-authoring mind, 15, 16, 52, 100, 102, 136
self-transforming mind, 15, 17, 100, 102, 136
socialized mind, 15, 16, 52, 53, 100, 102, 136

## P

Personality
  Big Five personality traits, 4, 41–42; dispositional variables, 4, 42
  extraversion (extrovert/extravert), 41, 42, 45
  introversion (Introvert); Myers-Briggs type indicator, 42n1; NEO PI-R, 106; traits, 44
Positive psychology, 12, 135, 136
Possible-selves, 4, 19, 22, 24, 25, 27–30, 69, 107
Psychoanalytic approach
  ego; id, 23; super ego, 23
Psychodynamic approach, 2, 4, 5, 24, 36, 89

## R

Risk aversion, 58–60, 111, 129

## S

Self-awareness
  self-concept, 28–30, 135
  self-identity, 16
Self-determination, 16, 66
Self-efficacy, 51, 55–57, 57n9, 60, 68, 109, 110
Self-esteem
  self-consistency motive, 53
  self-enhancement motive, 53

## T

Tolerance for ambiguity, 59–60, 111

## V

Values, 4, 6, 7, 9, 14n5, 16, 18, 19, 22, 24, 25, 31, 38, 42, 44, 53, 54, 61, 63–69, 75–77, 81, 83, 91, 92, 108, 112, 120, 121, 123, 124, 126, 127, 129, 131, 132

## W

Worldviews, 4, 19, 22, 24, 25, 31–40, 42, 57, 69, 108

Lightning Source UK Ltd.
Milton Keynes UK
UKHW012107120419
340941UK00005B/478/P